U.S. Policy Options for Iraq

A Reassessment

D1733016

Olga Oliker, Keith Crane, Audra K. Grant, Terrence K. Kelly, Andrew Rathmell, David Brannan

Prepared for the United States Air Force

Approved for public release; distribution unlimited

 PROJECT AIR FORCE

The research described in this report was sponsored by the United States Air Force under Contracts F49642-01-C-0003 and FA7014-06-C-0001. Further information may be obtained from the Strategic Planning Division, Directorate of Plans, Hq USAF.

Library of Congress Cataloging-in-Publication Data

U.S. policy options for Iraq : a reassessment / Olga Oliker ... [et al.].
   p. cm.
   Includes bibliographical references.
   ISBN 978-0-8330-4168-5 (pbk. : alk. paper)
   1. Iraq War, 2003– 2. United States—Politics and government—2001–
3. Iraq—Politics and government—2003– 4. Internal security—Iraq. 5. Iraq—
Economic conditions—21st century. I. Oliker, Olga. II. Rand Corporation.
III. Title: United States policy options for Iraq.

DS79.76.U28 2007
956.7044'31—dc22

2007022522

The RAND Corporation is a nonprofit research organization providing objective analysis and effective solutions that address the challenges facing the public and private sectors around the world. RAND's publications do not necessarily reflect the opinions of its research clients and sponsors.

RAND® is a registered trademark.

Cover photo: BAGHDAD, Iraq (AFPN) -- A member (bottom right) of the Combined Weapons Effectiveness Assessment Team assesses the impact point of a precision-guided 5,000-pound bomb through the dome of one of Saddam Hussein's key regime buildings here. The impact point is one of up to 500 the team will assess in coming weeks. (U.S. Air Force photo by Master Sgt. Carla Kippes)

Published 2007 by the RAND Corporation
1776 Main Street, P.O. Box 2138, Santa Monica, CA 90407-2138
1200 South Hayes Street, Arlington, VA 22202-5050
4570 Fifth Avenue, Suite 600, Pittsburgh, PA 15213-2665
RAND URL: http://www.rand.org/
To order RAND documents or to obtain additional information, contact
Distribution Services: Telephone: (310) 451-7002;
Fax: (310) 451-6915; Email: order@rand.org

Preface

In light of the continuing violence in Iraq, U.S. policymakers continue to reexamine policy options and their repercussions. This monograph assesses a number of approaches that the U.S. government can consider in its efforts to reduce sectarian violence and stabilize Iraq and presents recommendations that may help increase the likelihood of success. It also considers possible next steps to take, whether these efforts succeed or fail.

The monograph should be of interest to policymakers and analysts involved in international security and U.S. foreign policy, particularly U.S. policy toward Iraq. The analysis in this monograph is based on more than a year of research, which included travel to the region and extensive interviews with U.S., Iraqi, and other specialists, analysts, and officials, as one component of the project "The U.S. Air Force Role in the Middle East." It involved a multidisciplinary team of researchers who brought their expertise in political, economic, and military strategic analysis to these important questions. Readers of this monograph may also find the following RAND publications to be of interest:

- *America's Role in Nation-Building: From Germany to Iraq*, by James Dobbins, John G. McGinn, Keith Crane, Seth G. Jones, Rollie Lal, Andrew Rathmell, Rachel M. Swanger, and Anga Timilsina (MR-1753-RC, 2003)
- *Developing Iraq's Security Sector: The Coalition Provisional Authority's Experience*, by Andrew Rathmell, Olga Oliker, Terrence K. Kelly, David Brannan, and Keith Crane (MG-365-OSD, 2005)

- *The UN's Role in Nation-Building: From the Congo to Iraq*, by James Dobbins, Seth G. Jones, Keith Crane, Andrew Rathmell, Brett Steele, Richard Teltschik, and Anga Timilsina (MG-304-RC, 2005)
- *Insurgency and Counterinsurgency in Iraq*, by Bruce Hoffman (OP-127-IPC/CMEPP, 2004).

The research was sponsored by the Directorate for Operational Plans and Joint Matters, headquarters, U.S. Air Force (formerly AF/XOX, now A5X) and conducted within the Strategy and Doctrine Program of RAND Project AIR FORCE. The research for this report was completed in February 2007.

RAND Project AIR FORCE

RAND Project AIR FORCE (PAF), a division of the RAND Corporation, is the U.S. Air Force's federally funded research and development center for studies and analyses. PAF provides the Air Force with independent analyses of policy alternatives affecting the development, employment, combat readiness, and support of current and future aerospace forces. Research is conducted in four programs: Aerospace Force Development; Manpower, Personnel, and Training; Resource Management; and Strategy and Doctrine.

Additional information about PAF is available on our Web site: http://www.rand.org/paf/

Contents

Summary

Iraq is the most pressing foreign and security policy issue that the United States faces today. Continued failure to make Iraq stable and secure threatens to disrupt the Middle East not by catalyzing the spread of democracy but by exporting instability and conflict. If violence continues, Iraq's neighbors will use the country as a theater in which to pursue their own goals, including those at odds with Iraqi and U.S. interests. Iraq will remain a training ground for terrorist groups, threatening U.S. and allied security. Continued conflict in Iraq not only will remain extraordinarily costly in terms of U.S. lives and resources, but will also damage the credibility of the United States and the efficacy of U.S. forces. It also feeds perceptions around the world that the United States is engaged in a "war on Islam."

The U.S. government needs to consider alternative strategies and approaches for reducing the violence in Iraq. Even if policymakers choose not to make major changes, adjustments to current policies might help improve the effectiveness of the U.S. effort—though they can by no means guarantee success. The U.S. government should also begin considering next steps in Iraq in the event that the United States attains its policy goals and in the event that it does not.

Strategies

No effort to foster democracy and economic development in Iraq can succeed until the Iraqi people become more secure. Rising sectarian violence has supplanted insurgent and criminal violence as the greatest threat to Iraqis and to the future of the country. Putting an end to internecine violence demands policies different from those for defeating an insurgency alone: Reducing sectarian violence requires measures to prevent all groups from fighting, which differs from defeating an enemy. Incentives for undertaking violence as another form of politics must be reduced and eventually eliminated. No other effort or program will succeed unless violence is reduced.

Strategies the United States and its partners can undertake to reduce violence in Iraq fall into five broad categories:

1. Use overwhelming force to pacify the country and prevent further fighting.
2. Pick and support one or more "winners" of the civil war and help them gain control of Iraq, thus ending the conflict.
3. Help to partition Iraq into three separate states.
4. Leave Iraq and wait for one or more victors to emerge.
5. Maintain current efforts by seeking to broker a deal to reduce violence while Coalition troops focus on combating the insurgency and supporting the central government.

A force sufficient to subdue and disarm Iraq's many combatants would have to be much larger (perhaps a total of 350,000–500,000 troops) than current foreign troop levels permit. It would also have to be highly proficient at peace enforcement. Iraqi forces will not be capable of filling such a role any time soon. Outside the United States, there are not enough foreign forces that would operate under the necessary rules of engagement, that have the capabilities, and whose governments would be willing to deploy them to Iraq to do this job. Even in the United States, the government and military probably lack the political and military capacity to successfully pursue a strategy of overwhelming force at this time.

Choosing and backing winners would almost certainly backfire, whether the United States seeks to support a single ruler for Iraq or partition the country. The very decision to support a given faction could well destroy it politically. Moreover, picking a winner would run counter to U.S. goals for a unified, democratic Iraq. Partition, however carefully negotiated, and its aftermath would likely intensify, not reduce, sectarian violence. Although partition may be the outcome of continued war in Iraq, efforts to promote it on the part of the United States would not be good policy.

Leaving Iraq will not end sectarian strife and may stoke it. A U.S. departure could encourage combatants in potential future interventions to battle peace enforcers rather than to seek accommodation. For these reasons, if the U.S. presence prevents current levels of violence from worsening, an argument can be made for staying. However, the longer sectarian strife rises despite U.S. efforts, the more appealing the option of withdrawal becomes.

The U.S. mission in Baghdad has sought to broker a deal among the key factions to reduce sectarian violence. But, even though a national unity government has been created, its leaders represent sectarian interests and hold incompatible visions of Iraq's future. Although they all oppose violence in principle, some want to retain the capacity to use it in pursuit of their own ends. Moreover, the government does not incorporate all parties to the current fight, and many faction leaders do not control all the fighters in their factions. As violence continues, positions harden, and escalation and revenge make it harder to resolve disputes peacefully.

The Coalition is using the forces it has available to try to reduce sectarian violence. It has increased patrols in key regions, most notably Baghdad, utilizing Iraqi forces wherever possible. Recently, the United States has increased force levels in an effort to reduce violence in Baghdad. The U.S. mission has sought to include as many stakeholders as possible in the government and in discussions to reduce violence.

Because the other options do not appear likely to be implemented or to succeed, this current approach will likely continue until and unless violence escalates to the point that U.S. officials decide that withdrawal is preferable. Although we are not optimistic about success in the near term, as long as this continues to be the U.S. strategy, the tactics and approaches employed in pursuit of this overall strategy should be as effective as possible. We argue that an effective strategy must focus on reducing violence and ensuring that Iraqis are safe. This mission should be the first priority, taking precedence above all else. Better use of U.S.

forces, political suasion, diplomatic pressure, and aid dollars should all be geared to that goal for as long as U.S. efforts in Iraq continue. (See pp. 11–21.)

Political Policies

The United States can help prevent current levels of violence from rising by supporting a functioning national unity government, preventing a Kurdish takeover of Kirkuk, forestalling the formation of new autonomous regions, and ensuring that the central government continues to control oil revenue. Although U.S. influence on some issues is limited, it does have leverage with the Kurds. It also can use assistance and the influence it brings to strengthen central and provincial, rather than regional, authorities. The U.S. government also has some sway over international oil companies, which it should pressure to make their payments for oil through the central government.

Currently, Iraq's neighbors have chosen their own champions in the conflict. The United States should seek to discuss Iraq's future with all of Iraq's neighbors, including Syria and Iran. Discussions on reducing support for parties to the conflict and containing violence should begin on a bilateral basis but ideally expand to multilateral discussions and, eventually, a formal working group. Such a working group should include the United Kingdom, Japan, others interested in Iraq's stability, and the Iraqi government, as well as Iraq's neighbors. The U.S. government should also support regional and UN initiatives that show promise of reducing violence, even if the United States is not asked to participate directly in them. (See pp. 23–30.)

Security Policies

For violence in Iraq to be reduced, Iraq's own security forces must become less sectarian and more effective. Its Ministry of Interior (MoI), which has been implicated in a broad range of malfeasance and violence, must be thoroughly reformed. All security personnel should be vetted by commissions staffed by representatives of all parties. Hiring boards and complete lists of MoI employees need to be developed. Specialized police units should undergo thorough investigations; Coalition and Iraqi officials should investigate all complaints. They should make the results of these investigations public. Units with records of abuse should be disbanded. Individuals complicit in abuse, including high-level officials and those tied to them, must be brought to justice. (See pp. 31–36.)

Better financial controls are needed throughout the government to prevent government funds from flowing to militias and other violent groups. To control the flow of funds to militias, it is not enough to simply transfer all government payroll functions to the Ministry of Finance. In an atmosphere of corruption and nepotism, establishing systems of transparency and oversight will be the only way to attain any success. (See pp. 35, 41–43.)

Coalition forces should always patrol with Iraqi units—no non-Iraqi force should patrol alone, and Iraqi forces, too, should be accompanied by mentors if they are not patrolling jointly. Joint patrols will reduce the perception of foreign occupation, improve communication with the Iraqi populace, and constrain Iraqi forces from abusing their power. Whenever possible, Iraqi police must be visibly in the lead on patrols and should handle as many cases related to violence, irrespective of its origin, as possible. Coalition involvement, though likely still needed for some time to come, should be as subtle—and hidden from view—as possible. U.S. assistance should focus increasingly on mentoring the police and the army, especially by embedding more mentors within units at all levels and by bolstering local policing capacity. (See pp. 36–39, 43–44.)

The U.S. government should increase funding and support to assist Iraqi courts and prisons to function more effectively and in accordance with international standards. Absent progress in this area, improvements in the Iraqi police forces will have little effect. (See pp. 40–41.)

The U.S. government should focus its assistance programs and efforts on winning the hearts and minds of Iraqi citizens for the Iraqi government, not for the Coalition. Iraqi spokespeople and officials should speak first at press conferences and take the lead in providing information about the security situation in the country. (See pp. 45–46.)

Although the current Coalition focus on Baghdad is necessary to reduce violence, it is not sufficient, particularly if violence increases outside of Baghdad. If large numbers of troops continue to be needed to contain violence in Baghdad and if violence in other regions rises, the Coalition will have to send additional troops to Iraq to provide security to areas outside Baghdad—or accept failure in Iraq as a whole. We also recommend that, as long as combat operations continue, the joint force commander in Iraq consider curtailing air strikes, or at least the use of highly destructive weapons, in urban areas. (See p. 45.)

Economic Policies

To reduce the smuggling and resale of gasoline and diesel, which are primary sources of funding for insurgents and militias, the United States should press the Iraqi government to continue to raise, and eventually fully liberalize, the prices of these commodities. While price increases are never popular, a clear and transparent public information campaign can mitigate discontent. (See pp. 47–49.)

Improving and restructuring the operations of the oil ministry would result in increased production, exports, and government revenues. The U.S. government, in conjunction with the World Bank, should provide assistance in streamlining contracting procedures and encourage and provide technical assistance for restructuring the ministry along commercial lines, creating a professionally managed Iraqi national oil company. The U.S. government should also assist the Iraqi government in improving security for pipelines and terminals, in part by making greater use of private security providers and in part by improving the capabilities of Iraqi protective forces. (See pp. 49–52.)

While the United States should focus its assistance dollars on programs that can truly improve security, this should include appropriate spending to build the capacity of the Iraqi government to function and provide basic services. Programs to prevent the diversion of funds to militias and other violent actors are also worthy of support. Other assistance programs should be postponed until and unless security improves. The Iraqi government should take credit for results of assistance programs and be seen as the provider of government services. (See p. 53.)

If—and Only If—Violence Declines

If Coalition policies prove effective and violence declines, policies and programs should be adopted to make sure that a stabilized Iraq does not slip back into civil conflict. The United States and the international community should pledge their support for the inviolability of Iraq's borders and their commitment to Iraq's security. The U.S. government should commit to continuing to provide security assistance to Iraq. If the security situation stabilizes, demobilization, disarmament, and reintegration (DDR) programs should be undertaken to reduce and, eventually, disband militias and insurgent forces. As part of this process, a broad amnesty is advisable. The Iraqis may choose to engage in adjudication and reparations in conjunction with an amnesty, if peace becomes possible. However, such programs are not in the cards in the near future; at current levels of violence, they cannot work and would be a waste of resources. (See pp. 57–61.)

If peace breaks out, Iraq's intelligence services will need to be consolidated and restructured, along the lines initially envisioned for the Iraqi National Intelligence Service, with limited authority and appropriate oversight. (See pp. 61–62.)

A sharp decline in violence would also enable Iraq to pursue economic policies that would create a foundation for solid growth to cement stability. The U.S. government could usefully provide assistance to improve the operations of the electric power industry and make Iraq's welfare programs more effective. However, under any scenario, U.S. grant aid for infrastructure should end. Oil prices are sufficiently high that Iraq's oil sector should be self-financing. In other sectors, Iraq, like most other global aid recipients, should seek project loans, not grants, for investments in infrastructure. (See pp. 62–65.)

If Violence Fails to Decline

If U.S. and other Coalition forces cannot reduce the violence, pressure to withdraw troops will become more and more difficult to resist. The best measure of whether violence is rising or falling is the number of Iraqis killed each month. The U.S. government has recently increased troop levels, and U.S. officials will argue that the new approach needs time to work. It should, however, be clear by summer 2007 whether the recent surge has been effective in reducing the Iraqi death rate.

If the United States undertakes a withdrawal of its forces, it will have to be phased, and it will take time. But, well before deciding on a withdrawal, much less before beginning one, the United States should prepare to manage the repercussions of withdrawal and a continuing and expanding conflict in Iraq. These include the increased involvement of Iraq's neighbors in Iraq's affairs, escalating violence, and refugee flows.

U.S. policies could help mitigate these problems. First, U.S. forces should, to the extent possible, withdraw without haste once the withdrawal decision is made. The U.S. government should first consult with its allies, including the Iraqi government, concerning the advisability and means of withdrawal. Once it has made a decision, the U.S. government should inform the Iraqi government and public, its allies, and Iraq's neighbors of its plans. Second, friends and allies should be reassured that withdrawal does not mean that the United States plans to evacuate other bases or reduce its commitments to friends in the region. The U.S. government should assist neighbors, such as Jordan, to respond to any spillovers from the conflict in Iraq. The United States should work with the United Nations to pass a resolution recognizing Iraq's territorial integrity. The administration should be prepared to help Iraqi refugees, both by assisting neighboring countries and by arranging for Iraqis who worked for or helped the United States to emigrate. The United States should not seek to keep troops in any part of Iraq either to maintain control over oil fields, pipelines, and export terminals or to intervene in Iraq's future affairs. Once it has made a decision to withdraw, the U.S. government should adhere to that decision. Finally, future Iraqi governments may not be to the United

States' liking. Insofar as possible, however, the United States should seek appropriate relations with whatever Iraqi government (or governments) ultimately emerges. To the extent that Iraqi governments do not pursue policies antithetical to U.S. interests, the United States should consider continuing to provide assistance. (See pp. 67–74.)

Acknowledgments

We have a great many people to thank for their assistance in bringing this monograph to fruition. First of all, we would like to thank our project monitors at the former AF/XOX, particularly Lt. Col. William DeMaso, who helped guide this research. We are also grateful to colleagues at the Office of the Secretary of Defense, the Joint Staff, the U.S. Department of State, U.S. Central Command (USCENTCOM) (especially CDR John Couture), and U.S. Central Command Air Forces. We would like to thank many people in Baghdad who have worked at the U.S. embassy, other embassies, and the Iraq Reconstruction Management Office and the many Iraqis, both affiliated with the government and not, who were willing to share their thoughts. We also owe thanks to the many specialists and policymakers throughout the world who have been so generous with their time and their thoughts. In the course of our research, we were privileged to speak with people at the World Bank office in Amman; the U.S. embassy in Amman; the U.S. mission to NATO; the U.S. embassy in Brussels; the European Union Commission and Council; the French government; and academic analysts in Paris, Amman, and Haifa. They kindly provided their knowledge and perspectives, which richly informed our work. We would particularly like to thank RAND colleagues David E. Thaler, Bruce R. Pirnie, Derek Eaton, Sara A. Daly, Jerry M. Sollinger, Sarah Harting, and Nathan Chandler for assisting with this research effort. We also would like to thank the leadership of Project AIR FORCE, particularly Natalie W. Crawford, Andrew

Hoehn, David A. Shlapak, and David Ochmanek, for making this undertaking possible and supporting us throughout the project.

David C. Gompert, Michael O'Hanlon, and Karl P. Mueller reviewed earlier versions of this monograph. Their comments and suggestions made the final product a much better one. Kathryn Khamsi provided able assistance and support at several stages in the project. Francisco Walter and Hilary Wentworth provided important assistance at the closing stages of this effort. Lisa Bernard's skilled editing and Joanna Baker's shepherding through the process to completion are also greatly appreciated by the authors. Finally, our gratitude to all of the above in no way takes away from the fact that any errors, omissions, and mistakes in this monograph are the authors' alone.

Abbreviations

A5X	Directorate for Operational Plans and Joint Matters, headquarters, U.S. Air Force
AF/XOX	former abbreviation for Directorate for Operational Plans and Joint Matters, headquarters, U.S. Air Force
DDR	demobilization, disarmament, and reintegration
IMF	International Monetary Fund
INIS	Iraqi National Intelligence Service
IPS	Iraqi Police Service
mbd	million barrels per day
MNSTC-I	Multi-National Security Transition Command–Iraq
MoI	Ministry of Interior
PAF	Project AIR FORCE
PDS	Public Distribution System
PRT	Provincial Reconstruction Team
USAID	U.S. Agency for International Development
USCENTCOM	U.S. Central Command

CHAPTER ONE

Introduction

The Problem of Iraq

Iraq is the most pressing foreign and security policy issue facing the United States today. Continued failure to make Iraq stable and secure threatens to disrupt the Middle East not by catalyzing the spread of democracy but by exporting instability and conflict. If violence continues, Iraq's neighbors will use the country as a theater in which to pursue their own goals, including those at odds with the interests of Iraq and the United States. Iraq will remain a training ground for terrorist groups, threatening U.S. and allied security. Continued conflict in Iraq not only will remain extraordinarily costly in terms of U.S. lives and resources, but will also damage the United States' credibility and the efficacy of U.S. forces. It also feeds perceptions around the world that the United States is engaged in a "war on Islam."

Official statements concerning U.S. policy goals in Iraq remain much as they were when U.S. forces invaded the country in March 2003: to create a secure, democratic state with a vibrant market economy that poses no threat to its neighbors. Prospects for successfully attaining these goals have dimmed, eroded by the insurgency, escalating internecine violence, and rising rates of violent crime, including kidnappings and murder.

Suggestions for new policies concerning Iraq have come fast and furious in fall 2006 and winter 2007, ranging from deploying large numbers of new U.S. forces to rapid withdrawal. Even if the administration decides not to make major changes to its overall strategy, current policies can be improved. This monograph presents recommendations designed to reduce the level of violence against Iraqis—in our view, the goal that the U.S. government should give the highest priority. It should gear political, security, and economic policies to attaining this goal.

Even if current policies remain unchanged, the U.S. government should prepare now for the repercussions of either success or failure. If security improves, a new package of policies will be needed to cement the improved status quo. If U.S. goals are not attained, violence continues or escalates, and the U.S. forces are withdrawn, the U.S. government needs to plan now to mitigate the consequences of withdrawal.

The monograph begins with an analysis of the current security situation in Iraq. It then discusses the broad strategic options available to the United States and others given the evolution of Iraq to date. Next, it presents ways to improve current policies if policymakers choose not to make substantial changes at this time, assessing how policies can be made most effective given political and resource constraints. The monograph then turns to steps that would need to be taken if this effort is successful. It concludes by discussing the issues and options the United States must consider in the event that the level of violence fails to fall.

The Situation Today

If violence remains at current levels in Iraq, the U.S. government will fail to achieve its goals for the country: Not only will Iraq not be secure, democratic, or prosperous, but the violence will threaten the stability of Iraq's neighbors. Levels of violence in Iraq today are so high that they threaten Iraq's existence as a state. The United Nations reports that violence killed more than 2,000 Iraqis each month between February 2006 and the end of that year. More than 3,400 died in each of July, October, and November 2006. Iraq Body Count[1] estimates that between 54,211 and 59,868 Iraqis were killed between the start of

---

[1]   Iraq Body Count is an independent effort to estimate Iraqi civilian casualties and where they occur, on the basis of media reports.

the war and January 19, 2007.[2] Other estimates are even higher. The dozens of bombings, assassinations, and other attacks each month not only kill but also maim thousands.[3]

Iraqis, especially those living in Baghdad and in predominantly Sunni areas, find current levels of violence overwhelming.[4] In March and June 2006, poll results released by the International Republican Institute found that 93 percent of Iraqis felt that security was unsatisfactory; three-quarters of respondents described security as poor.[5] Because of the prevalence of violence, Iraqi adults restrict their activities, children are kept home from school, and families and friends organize patrols to make their neighborhoods safer. The United Nations estimates that there are up to 1.8 million Iraqi refugees outside the country and 1.6 million displaced persons within it, for a total of more than 3 million displaced persons in and from a country of slightly more than 27 million.[6] Although many people were displaced before the war began and large numbers of Iraqis began to return home in 2003 and 2005, this trend has now reversed, as thousands of Iraqis flee the country daily.[7] This has immediate and long-lasting effects on the economy and the operations of the government.

U.S. efforts to foster democracy and economic development in Iraq cannot succeed until and unless security is improved. The current lack of security in Iraq places a binding constraint on economic growth. Although the United States has highlighted economic development as a goal and economic growth in Iraq is important for raising Iraqi living standards, economic assistance will not create conditions for sustained economic growth as long as the security environment is so dismal. Because of the lack of security, the United States has had difficulty in translating its assistance into improvements in living stan-

---

[2] Iraq Body Count (undated); see also Brookings Institution (undated).

[3] Brookings Institution (undated).

[4] International Republican Institute (2006).

[5] International Republican Institute (2006); Brookings Institution (undated).

[6] Brookings Institution (undated).

[7] UNHCR (undated); Brookings Institution (undated).

dards and public services. The record of U.S. aid and reconstruction efforts to date has been poor, in part because the violence has so hampered reconstruction. The institutional weaknesses of the Iraqi government and mistaken assistance policies on the part of the United States have compounded difficulties in providing aid effectively.[8] Although improvements in aid programs can be identified, until and unless levels of violence in Iraq are reduced, neither assistance directed at making Iraq more democratic and the government more capable nor that designed to improve the economic well-being of Iraqis is likely to have much impact.

Measures to stop the violence will be effective only if they address the sources of violence. Broadly speaking, these sources fall into four categories:

1. *Sectarian violence*: violence perpetrated by religious or political groups for political reasons or other reasons pertaining to the interests of the group, such as revenge for past injustices.[9] Sectarian assassinations in Baghdad and the conflicts between Shia groups in Al Basrah fall into this category.

2. *Ideological violence*: violence designed to force a change in the ideological complexion of the Iraqi regime, including by those who seek to install a system rooted in Islamic law or to thwart

---

[8] An example is the focus on investing in new electric power–generating capacity without improving the operations of the electricity ministry. Because managers have few incentives to run the system efficiently, maintenance and repairs are neglected, contributing to poor service. Because Iraqi households get power for free (when available), they face no incentives to conserve. Thus, large investments in the sector have not succeeded in ensuring a continuous supply of power. The failure to improve the supply of power, especially in Baghdad, remains one of the main grievances of Iraqis. See the quarterly reports from the Office of the Special Inspector General for Iraq Reconstruction for detailed assessments of the various problems that have plagued U.S. assistance efforts in Iraq. The most recent, the twelfth such report (Office of the Special Inspector General for Iraq Reconstruction, 2007, pp. 4–5) itemizes problems with programs to reduce corruption, improve infrastructure security, and coordinate assistance efforts.

[9] We refer to this form of violence as *sectarian* whether or not the groups are religiously motivated, indicating by this term violence linked to disputes based on ethnicity, religion, or clan.

U.S. policy goals, epitomized by the activities of al Qaeda in Iraq.

3. *Nationalist violence*: attacks on Coalition forces to compel the U.S. military to leave Iraq, a primary motivation for many who have joined the Sunni insurgency.

4. *Criminal violence*: armed robbery, extortion, kidnappings for money, and other criminal activities designed to raise money, or the resort to murder to settle disputes.

These categories overlap. Ideological, nationalist, or sectarian goals are often intertwined. Criminals sell arms—including anti-aircraft missiles—to insurgent groups and kidnap Iraqi citizens and foreigners for money. Although their motivations may not be political, the violence that their actions support often is.

Until recently, most Iraqis who live outside Baghdad or the more violent cities of Al Anbar province have been more affected by crime and general lawlessness than by the danger of insurgent attack. Nationalist actors have consistently targeted Iraqi security personnel throughout the country because Iraqi forces are viewed as complicit in the occupation. Increasingly, however, sectarian violence presents the greatest problem.

The rise in sectarian violence is both an indicator and a cause of the increasing division of Iraqi society along ethnic and religious lines. This phenomenon has steadily gathered force since the U.S. invasion. The sectarian nature of voting in the January 2005 elections was repeated in the December 2005 elections.[10] Ethnic cleansing and clashes between ethnic groups have also been common since shortly after the war began.[11] In 2006, however, sectarian violence and perceptions of it have worsened: Some 425,000 Iraqis fled their homes between January and mid-November 2006, according to United Nations estimates,

---

[10] Iraqi election results are available on the Web site of the Independent Electoral Commission of Iraq (undated); see also Marr (2006).

[11] A variety of news outlets have covered this aspect of the violence. A representative sampling includes Clover (2003), Basu (2003), Cambanis (2005), Poole (2005), and Youssef and al Dulaimy (2005).

as a result of ethnic cleansing. The rate of internal displacement in the middle of that year was some 50,000 people per month.[12] Ethnic cleansing in Kirkuk, Baghdad, and other areas and the growth of sectarian attacks on individuals and communities indicate that the focus of violence in Iraq has now shifted from attacks on Coalition forces to an internecine struggle.[13]

If *civil war* is "a war between opposing groups of citizens of the same country,"[14] then Iraq is embroiled in a civil war, one that has worsened throughout 2006. Whatever one chooses to call the current conflict, Iraqi-on-Iraqi violence is more dangerous for the stability of Iraq than are insurgent attacks on Coalition forces. Iraqi-on-Iraqi attacks feed on each other, escalating the violence. Attacks on groups increase allegiance to those groups, involving more and more of the population in the struggle. If Iraqi-on-Iraqi violence is not reduced, civil war will continue and escalate, the central government will lose even more control, and Iraq will continue on the path to becoming a failed state.

Iraq's leaders contribute to the problem. Although a national unity government has been created, the leaders of this government pursue sectarian interests rather than cooperate. They have failed to take concerted actions to reduce the violence among Iraq's ethnic and religious groups.[15]

The members of Iraq's government continue to hold incompatible visions of Iraq's future. Many among Iraq's ruling parties see themselves as the emergent leaders of Iraq and do not want to share power. The factions also disagree about the extent to which Iraq should be

---

[12] UNHCR (undated).

[13] Windawi and Barnes (2006); Walker (2006); "Ramadan Bomb Targets Shiites" (2006); Jervis (2006).

[14] Merriam-Webster (undated).

[15] As Shiites seek to cement control, Kurds to solidify autonomy, and Sunnis to protect themselves, government officials representing these sects accuse each other, often credibly, of carrying out targeted assassinations. Numerous successive efforts to create a consolidated way forward, such as the October 2006 Mecca 10-point declaration by Sunni and Shia stakeholders or the December 2006 national reconciliation conference, have failed due to noninvolvement or nonimplementation by key actors. See, for example, the discussions in Cordesman and Davies (2007) and in International Crisis Group (2006c).

secular or democratic. Others seek more autonomy or more power for their regions or people, more autonomy than other Iraqis wish to give. Most Iraqi Kurds, for example, including some in the leadership, aspire to an independent Kurdistan. Although Kurdish leaders may feel that independence is not possible at present and support and take part in the Iraqi government as a result, independence remains an important goal.[16]

Although these leaders may, in principle, oppose the use of violence to attain these goals, some also wish to retain the capacity to use violence. They have seen that, in some instances, violence can be successfully employed to achieve their goals; violence is viewed as a viable strategy. Negotiations have had little history of success in Iraq. Not surprisingly, some Iraqi leaders see violence as more likely to achieve their goals than elections and compromise.

In light of the dangers to the stability of Iraq, the key mission of the Coalition should be to significantly reduce levels of sectarian violence, ending the civil war. All aspects of U.S. and Iraqi policy should focus on achieving this objective. Policies designed to fight insurgency, reduce day-to-day crime, and build government institutions should be tailored not only to be effective in an atmosphere of worsening sectarian violence, but also to ensure that they contribute to its reduction.

Building institutions is difficult under any conditions; when a country is embroiled in conflict, the task is even more difficult. Institutions become distorted because domestic groups and actors see the government as an instrument and source of resources to fuel their sectarian objectives. While the United States and other donors work to create institutions and policies that discourage corruption, Iraqi officials see diverting government funds to support their backers as necessary for their groups' survival—and for potential victory over others. These officials make appointments to office based on ethnic or religious allegiances and thus build strong sectarian coalitions within the government. Individuals are recruited to high-level positions because of group affiliation rather than competence. In this environment, police

---

[16] See International Crisis Group (2004, 2006b). This is also borne out by the authors' conversations with Iraqi citizens.

involvement in assassinations and kidnappings, murders of and threats to attorneys and judges, and the implication of detention centers in torture (Coalition forces have repeatedly found clear evidence of torture at Iraqi prison facilities) take on a sectarian tinge.[17] Security forces become training grounds for the parties to the civil war.

Not only do Iraqi security forces fail to provide security; they have become part of the problem. Sunnis are increasingly underrepresented in the security forces, though with some variation by region.[18] Some Sunni soldiers have refused to serve away from their home regions.[19] Clashes between units composed of different ethnic groups have been reported.[20] Police units have reportedly engaged in assassinations and kidnappings for both pecuniary and political advantage.[21] If the civil war worsens, even more Iraqi security forces will likely become sectarian combatants.

Widespread sectarian violence changes the mission of Coalition forces. While Coalition forces will continue to combat insurgents and al Qaeda operatives, the key mission must now be to put an end to internecine violence. This mission creates different requirements from those for counterinsurgency operations. Whereas counterinsurgency is about defeating an enemy (though the insurgency in Iraq was always composed of a number of different enemies), peace enforcement among rival groups requires stopping all groups from fighting, not just defeating one set of combatants.[22]

---

[17] For documentation on these issues, see International Crisis Group (2006a), U.S. Department of Defense (2006), and Cordesman and Davies (2007).

[18] Castaneda (2006); Youssef (2006). Historically, they were better represented in the army officer corps than in other organizations, but recent reports suggest that their numbers there are now dwindling as well (author discussions with U.S. and Iraqi officials, 2006–2007).

[19] Hernandez (2006).

[20] Filkins, Mahmood, and al-Ansary (2006).

[21] Zavis (2006); Moore (2006a).

[22] The term *peace enforcement operations* is defined by the U.S. Joint Chiefs of Staff (1995, p. III-13) as "the application of military force, or threat of its use, normally pursuant to international authorization, to compel compliance with regulations or sanctions designed to maintain or restore peace and order."

The current mission in Iraq is primarily a peace enforcement mission, and all involved must see it as such. This affects how military operations are conducted and what political actions are taken. The core questions become how to make peace in a way that is lasting and in a way that contributes to reducing or eliminating other forms of violence as well. This is not an impossible task: Many societies have emerged from civil war and built effective government institutions, even democratic institutions, both on their own and with the aid of others.

Iraq has a few things going for it despite the rising violence. It has an educated, capable population and a history of academic and scientific achievement. Some pockets of Iraq enjoy relative peace and security. The United States, its allies, and all of Iraq's neighbors want to keep Iraq together; none wishes to see it dismembered. Most importantly, Iraq's people remain committed to their future, even under the current circumstances. Based on public opinion polls and the turnout for the December and January 2005 elections, most Iraqis continue to support a national unity government and some form of democracy.[23] But, as sectarian divides deepen and become more violent, Iraqis' goals for their country's future are likely to embody more and more separation along ethnic, tribal, and sectarian lines. Significantly reducing sectarian violence soon is essential to Iraq's future.

Iraq is hampered by having no history of good government or strong institutions divorced from historical and ethnic divides. Efforts to support capacity-building and reform in these areas have been undertaken but have made limited progress. Iraq's security institutions, particularly the interior and defense ministries, remain incapable of sustaining and, in many cases, controlling the forces under their purview.[24]

The capacity of the United States to improve on this record is mixed. On the one hand, the United States brings great military, financial, and political resources to assist the Iraqi government in quelling the violence. It is the outside actor that can plausibly be expected to undertake the effort of enforcing peace. On the other hand, the

---

[23] International Republican Institute (2006).

[24] Author discussions with U.S., coalition, and Iraqi personnel (2003–2007).

United States is not seen as an honest broker in Iraq. Many, perhaps most, Iraqis perceive the problems Iraq faces as the fault of the United States. The Iraqi population assumed that reconstruction would follow closely on the heels of Saddam's defeat. In the words of one senior Iraqi leader who played a major role in the resistance against Saddam, "We thought that, if you could defeat Saddam in three weeks [sic], you would rebuild the country in three months."[25] According to this official, the Coalition's failure to do so was attributed to conscious U.S. design rather than to ineptitude. Today, Iraqis continue to view their country as under U.S. control; many feel that the United States has intentionally plunged Iraq into violence.

---

[25] Author discussion (March 2004).

CHAPTER TWO

Defining and Assessing Alternative Strategies for Iraq

In light of the trends and levels of violence in Iraq and the increasingly sectarian nature of that violence, strategies for future action on the part of the United States and its partners fall into five broad categories. While some of these options are, prima facie, more appealing than others, they represent the broad spectrum of what can be done:

1. Use overwhelming force to pacify the country and prevent further fighting.
2. Pick and support one or more "winners" of the civil war and help them to gain control of Iraq, thus ending the conflict.
3. Partition Iraq into three separate states.
4. Leave Iraq and wait for one or more victors to emerge.
5. Maintain current efforts by seeking to broker a deal to reduce violence while Coalition troops focus on combating the insurgency and supporting the central government.

Employ Overwhelming Force

Employing overwhelming force is the critical component of a successful peace enforcement operation. When local forces are unreliable, as they are in Iraq, and local political actors are incapable of delivering peace, overwhelming force by an outside power, which patrols the streets and is able to face down combatants, restores security by effectively deterring further violence.

By taking away the effectiveness of violent action by the various factions, overwhelming force can bring combatants to the table to negotiate a political solution. Once such a solution is negotiated, the foreign force helps enforce the agreement until local security forces loyal to the government, not one or another of the quarreling factions, become sufficiently strong to provide security themselves. Overwhelming force has been successfully used to stop a number of conflicts, including those in Bosnia, Sierra Leone, and Liberia.

For the force to be overwhelming, to be able to subdue and disarm the many combatants in Iraq, it would have to be very large. Estimates cited at the start of the conflict and based on the troop-to-population ratios of successful operations, suggested that 350,000 to 500,000 troops would be necessary to provide security, even before sectarian violence grew.[1] Daniel Byman and Kenneth Pollack estimate that 450,000 troops would be needed to quell "all-out" civil war in Iraq.[2] These numbers are all based on troop-to-population ratios. With an Iraqi population of slightly more than 27 million, to reach a Balkans-level troop ratio of 20 soldiers for every 1,000 inhabitants, more than 500,000 troops would be needed. If the "surge" announced by the U.S. President in January 2007 is implemented as planned, there will be a total of some 175,000 foreign forces in Iraq.

Some might argue that high troop levels are needed only in the most violent parts of the country. The ratios on which this research is based are taken from cases in which violence was not uniform across the territory at issue. In those countries, troops were more concentrated in some areas than others. Consequently, the estimated numbers for Iraq are broadly appropriate. Moreover, even if one sought a ratio of 20 troops to 1,000 civilians for Baghdad, a city of about 6 million, 120,000 troops would be required for Baghdad alone.

Raising troop levels would be difficult for the United States because U.S. armed forces are already heavily committed and strained by the high operational tempo required by deployments in Afghani-

---

[1]   Dobbins, McGinn, et al. (2003).

[2]   Byman and Pollack (2006).

stan, Iraq, and elsewhere in the world.[3] Growing political opposition to the war would make large-scale force increases unpopular. Even if the will existed for a very large increase in overall U.S. force size so as to support greater deployments to Iraq, recruiting, training, and deploying new forces would take time—time during which conflict in Iraq would continue and intensify.

At increased force levels below the ratios needed to forcibly pacify the country, it is unlikely that the United States and its allies would be able to quell violence; they may simply draw more of it on themselves. The Coalition countries are not viewed as honest brokers in Iraq. U.S. and UK soldiers have been accused and convicted of atrocities, and some parties to the conflict, such as Muqtada al-Sadr, claim that the U.S. presence is the cause of internecine conflict.[4] In such an environment, a more active Coalition role could lead to more violence and greater public support for anti-Coalition forces. Warring groups might form an alliance of convenience against the Coalition. Such cooperation would almost certainly be short-lived, but it could result in significant casualties for Coalition forces while it lasted.

One solution to this problem is to achieve the necessary troop levels by using local personnel. The effort to train Iraqi forces to take over the task of fighting the insurgency and keeping the peace is nearly as old as the conflict itself. But Iraqi forces have consistently lacked the numbers and capability to succeed in these missions. As sectarian divides have deepened within the population, these fissures have been reflected among Iraqi security personnel. The result is split loyalties. Individuals may fight at the command of the national government, but they may also be fighting in the interests of their own sectarian groups—either concurrently or in separate actions. When units or even individual soldiers from one ethnic or regional group take part in operations outside their home region or group, they are often viewed as aggressors attacking the other population, further deepening sectarian divides. Sunni populations, in particular, have developed not unrea-

---

[3] See Davis et al. (2005).

[4] Ridolfo (2006); Bartholet (2006); Enders (2006).

sonable fears of attacks by police and other security services dominated by the Shia.

The goal of creating national Iraqi security forces loyal to the government rather than to sectarian leaders remains, but few units of the current force reflect such loyalties. Meanwhile, it has become increasingly difficult to foster national loyalties under the current conditions of rising intergroup violence.

If current Coalition forces are insufficient and Iraqi forces are not capable, some other outside actor, either supranational, such as the United Nations, or composed of willing states other than the current Coalition partners, could be called on to field the necessary force.

But few countries are likely to risk their soldiers in Iraq as part of what would be a highly dangerous mission. Getting enough forces willing to do what must be done is, at the time of this writing, an insurmountable challenge. Of those countries that might provide forces, many would do so only under restrictive rules of engagement. This would make it all but impossible to effectively impose peace on warring factions. Even with permissive rules of engagement, few forces other than the current Coalition or major European countries have the capability to carry out such a mission effectively. Thus, any solution calling for overwhelming force would entail a much larger U.S. troop presence—with all of the problems that presents.

Pick, and Back, Winners

This option has a long and storied history. Backing a particular faction or factions to help them defeat their enemies is a time-honored and time-tested mechanism of putting an end to conflict and, at least in theory, placing a loyal and beholden friend in charge.[5] However, as modern weaponry has become easier to obtain and combatants have

---

[5] During the period of the Raj, the UK successfully picked and backed local groups to expand and consolidate its authority in India. It followed a similar approach in Iraq between 1920 and 1932 under the British Mandate. Coalition forces generally and successfully supported the Bosnians in the bedlam of the mid-1990s. Less successfully, the United States fought alongside the South Vietnamese in Vietnam.

become more mobile, sustainable success in such endeavors has become more elusive. The long-term subjugation of one group by another is increasingly difficult to sustain: The defeated party can field an effective insurgency that the dominant group finds impossible to suppress. Conflicts in Sri Lanka and the Philippines, among others, show how difficult it can be to suppress an aggrieved minority. In Iraq, a strategy of picking winners would be unlikely to lead to a desirable end state.

The choice facing the United States would be to ally with one or more Shia groups or with one or more Sunni groups. There is no other viable "side" to take in Iraq; "aligning" with the Kurds would leave open the conflict between the others. In either case, victory would involve mass killings. Even if the United States sought to constrain its ally, failures to stop such activities would occur—and would implicate the United States. Aside from the moral repercussions of being associated with such atrocities, U.S. legislation prohibits U.S. assistance to forces that are credibly accused of human rights abuses. Backing a faction in this conflict could well become illegal. It would also damage U.S. credibility as it seeks to advance the goals of democratization, human rights, and accountability globally.

The very decision to choose a group to support could well backfire. Hostility to the presence of foreign forces in Iraq, especially U.S. forces, would probably increase and redound to the detriment of the faction supported by the United States. Masking U.S. backing would be impossible. If the U.S.-backed faction failed, the United States would have a clear enemy at the helm of Iraq.

Even if the United States could choose and back a winning side, the results could well be detrimental to U.S. interests. The U.S. government has strongly supported a unified, democratic Iraq and a negotiated settlement to the conflict. If the U.S. government were to abandon these positions and choose a "winner," to annihilate opposition, Iraq would very likely return to the patterns of the past, with a new dictator coming to power. The historical record suggests that attempting to back a winner may not yield a reliable partner; today's ally all too frequently becomes tomorrow's foe.[6] Moreover, the weaker side would likely continue the insurgency, perpetuating the conflict for many years.

Partition

Partition of Iraq into three states, dominated, respectively, by Sunni, Shia, and Kurdish populations and leaders, has a certain appeal. Under one proposal, U.S. senator and presidential candidate Joseph Biden and Council on Foreign Relations president emeritus Leslie Gelb argue for the creation of highly autonomous regions, rather than de jure separate states.[7] Partition's advantages seem logical: Each of the major sectarian groups in Iraq would have a state. Factionalized forces could fight for their "own" people rather than feigning loyalty to an Iraqi state that seems increasingly illegitimate.

Partition may, in fact, be the eventual outcome of the war in Iraq, but it is not an outcome for which the United States should wish—or try to effect. U.S. support for the partition of Iraq would be viewed, rightly, as an abandonment of its support of Iraq's unity government and hopes for a democratic future. These may no longer be possible to support, given the extent of violence, but, by throwing its weight behind partition, the United States might engender at least as much violence for at least as long as it would if it tried to choose a side.

Although Iraq does have three major sectarian groups (as well as a few smaller ones), the groups are not neatly divided geographically, as the ethnic cleansing already under way demonstrates. Not only is Baghdad itself ethnically mixed—so are towns and cities throughout the country. The division of Iraq would precipitate even more ethnic cleansing than has taken place to date, displacing ethnic populations and triggering more killings. However carefully partition were to be negotiated, groups would wind up dissatisfied, and each would believe that the U.S. and other Coalition forces had backed one or another of

---

[6]   Manuel Noriega in Panama, Mobutu Sese Seko in the Democratic Republic of the Congo, and Saddam Hussein in Iraq, among others, went from being U.S. friends to U.S. enemies.

[7]   Biden and Gelb (2006).

their enemies. Fighting over ethnically mixed areas would intensify, further feeding sectarian conflict. The more Coalition forces became involved in the fighting, the more hostility toward them would grow. The United States would likely be held at least partly responsible for the atrocities that would ensue from partition.

Whether or not partition would be successful, it would create and heighten animosities and territorial claims among Iraq's population that would last for generations. This would increase the potential for future conflict, either between Iraq's successor states, if partition came to pass, or within Iraq itself, if it did not.

If partition were to succeed, the successor states would be weak and require significant support to become viable. Neighbors such as Iran and Saudi Arabia might see "Shiastan" and "Sunnistan" as client states and potentially foster conflict between them. The Kurds would seek U.S. help to maintain independence and to gain and retain control of key oil fields and transport routes. If the United States were to grant this support, it would be seen as an enemy by the other two successors, perhaps provoking a potentially dangerous intervention by Turkey, Syria, and Iran, which, with sizable Kurdish populations of their own, have much to lose and nothing to gain from an independent Kurdistan. Turkey might move forces into the area, as it has done in the past. If the United States failed to support the Kurds, Kurdistan would probably become a failed state. Efforts by the United States to evenhandedly support and aid all three successor states would be unlikely to be perceived as evenhanded by any parties, inside or outside Iraq. These efforts would put the United States at odds with Saudi Arabia, Turkey, and Iran.

It is difficult to see how efforts to partition Iraq would not lead to more, rather than less, violence. Partition would also likely lead to more involvement by neighboring states in Iraq. Continued conflict might well spill over into neighboring states.

Leave

If overwhelming force would be infeasible and picking a winner or partition would likely lead to outcomes detrimental to U.S. and Iraqi interests, the United States may be best served by withdrawing its troops. The strongest argument against withdrawal is that U.S. and other Coalition forces are preventing a bad situation from becoming worse. Those who argue that U.S. forces must remain in Iraq predict that their departure would cause even greater violence, followed by the creation of terrorist safe havens and an arena in which Iraq's neighbors would vie for influence.[8] Some argue that withdrawal would have high costs in terms of a loss in U.S. credibility.[9] They say that withdrawal might encourage insurgents elsewhere to battle forces, U.S. or not, engaged in peace enforcement operations rather than to seek accommodation with domestic foes. They also believe that withdrawal would reduce U.S. credibility with current or potential partners or allies around the globe, as the United States would be perceived as not adhering to its commitments.[10] The credibility of promises by the United States to defend Arab states, especially those situated around the Persian Gulf, is of particular concern. Opponents of withdrawal also cite the dangers posed to other U.S. policy interests. Withdrawal from Iraq could be viewed as reinforcing perceptions that Iran has bested the United States in Iraq and is in a position of rising regional power.[11] Some argue that withdrawal would set back the attainment of U.S. goals of a peaceful Middle East and the spread of democracy in the region.[12]

---

[8] See, for example, Klein (2006), "Between Staying and Going" (2006), and White House (2006b).

[9] In President George W. Bush's remarks at a Republican Party event in Nashville, Tennessee, in August 2006, the President said that early departure would "shred the credibility of the United States of America" (White House, 2006a).

[10] In his December 18, 2005, address to the nation, President George W. Bush said, regarding withdrawal, "We would abandon our Iraqi friends and signal to the world that America cannot be trusted to keep its word" (White House, 2005).

[11] Charles Krauthammer (2006) makes this argument.

[12] Krauthammer (2006).

Each of these arguments has weaknesses. Credibility is not enhanced by adhering to a losing strategy; nor are other U.S. goals in the Middle East. Iraq has already become a training ground for terrorists and a cause célèbre for radical Islamists. U.S. withdrawal would eliminate a primary draw for foreign fighters—the opportunity to fight against and kill Americans.

If U.S. forces were to leave, Iran would see the U.S. departure as vindication. As conflict continues, the Iranian government would likely find itself increasingly involved in Iraq. It might even attempt to pacify the country, encountering some, if not all, of the same problems as the United States. It would certainly have to deal with an influx of refugees and could possibly suffer from the spread of the conflict to Kurdish or Arab enclaves in Iran itself. Under this scenario, Tehran might well come to regret the U.S. departure.

The departure of U.S. troops will not end sectarian strife and may well exacerbate it. Iraq's neighbors could be drawn into the conflict, as they assist internal allies. Insofar as it keeps violence from getting worse and prevents groups such as al Qaeda in Iraq from securing a stronghold in that country, a continued U.S. presence may be beneficial. However, the longer that sectarian strife continues despite U.S. efforts to quell it, the more difficult it will be to avoid withdrawing U.S. forces.

Maintain Current Efforts

Current U.S. policy relies on a continuing effort to broker a deal among key factions to reduce, and eventually eliminate, political violence, while attacking groups perceived as spoilers. This strategy has not worked, in great part because Iraq's leaders are hedging against the failure of a unified Iraq by seeking to ensure the security of their own ethnic and religious groups. The persistent efforts of all parties to buttress their own positions contribute to the violence and to the likelihood that Iraq will fail.

Even if all the political leaders participating in Iraq's current government sought to halt the violence, they might be unsuccessful. The national unity government does not represent all the factions that fight. Leaders of the represented factions often do not control all fighters in their factions. These leaders might seek to end the violence but are unable to deliver. Those not sitting at the table are unlikely to abandon violence as a tool to achieve their goals.

As the violence continues, positions harden; fewer people see a political solution as plausible. Escalation and revenge have already set in; retaliatory killings are commonplace. In this atmosphere, a moratorium on all killings may be the right solution, but it is not an appealing one to the many who feel wronged and who desire vengeance. As violence continues, a deal will become harder to strike.

To make violence less appealing both to political leaders and to fighters, it must be made less effective. In pursuit of this goal, U.S. and other Coalition forces have sought to support the national unity government by training Iraqi security forces, increasing patrols in Baghdad and elsewhere, and, as of January 2007, increasing U.S. force commitments in Iraq for an unknown period of time.

From Strategy to Policy

The United States is faced with a portfolio of unappealing options, many of which appear to have little chance of producing positive results. Troop increases to levels deemed necessary according to U.S. experience in other conflicts seem impossible. Partition or the backing of a faction would likely exacerbate the violence and increase the involvement of Iraq' neighbors in the conflict. Administration officials have stated that large-scale troop reductions are not on the table.[13] While the current approach of efforts to broker a deal and reduce violence with the troops and policy tools available is fraught with problems, it is likely to remain U.S. policy at least until early 2009.

If the broad outlines of the strategy are to continue, we argue that parts of it, at least, can be improved, making it more likely, although still far from guaranteed, that violence will decline and the Iraqi gov-

---

[13] Pfeiffer (2006).

ernment will become more viable. For this strategy to be improved, the reduction of violence must become the central focus of U.S. efforts in Iraq. Traditional assistance programs try to accelerate economic growth, enhance democracy, and improve government operations—policy goals that the U.S. government has articulated for Iraq. U.S. assistance programs were instrumental in successfully holding three elections: two parliamentary and a referendum on the constitution. But elections have not dampened the violence nor have U.S. reconstruction programs, hobbled as they have been by the costs and inefficiencies caused by the lack of security. Economic development programs and efforts to foster civil society have also not had a notable impact. The growing violence has been a principal reason that these efforts have had such limited success.

While sectarian violence has emerged as the most critical threat to Iraq's future and reducing it is the most crucial task facing the Coalition, all forms of violence must decline if Iraq is to become a viable state. The forms of violence are interdependent; a decline in one will contribute to a decline in others. If sectarian violence drops, the climate for criminal activity and insurgents will become less hospitable. If crime declines, the environment for sectarian or ideological violence will become less accommodating, making it easier to treat all violence as criminal and decreasing the availability of weapons for cash.

Although U.S. efforts to date have not been particularly successful, the U.S. government retains a number of policy tools to combat violence in Iraq; the way in which they are employed could be improved. The use of U.S. military forces is the most prominent among these policy tools, but political suasion, diplomatic pressure on Iraq's neighbors, security assistance, and economic aid can also be useful, if applied effectively. In the chapters that follow, we provide recommendations on how policies in each of these areas can be better utilized to combat violence.

CHAPTER THREE

Political Suasion

Two key policies in the political sphere create the necessary, though far from sufficient, preconditions for helping stabilize Iraq and reduce violence. First of these is continuing support for the Iraqi national unity government. Without such a government, Iraq will fail. Second is the need to engage Iraq's neighbors in efforts to reduce support for groups engaged in violence in Iraq.

Maintain a National Unity Government

The formation of the national unity government was a crucial step in curbing sectarian violence, albeit not a sufficient one. A national unity government is far more likely to pursue peace than one excluding major parties to the conflict. The current government makes reconciliation possible not because of the particular individuals at its helm but because it includes representatives spanning the major sectarian and ethnic divides in Iraq. Another government that is as or more representative would be no less acceptable.

But a national unity government must surmount three major, near-term challenges if it is to survive and succeed:

1. Prevent a Kurdish takeover of Kirkuk.
2. Prevent the creation of additional regions.
3. Ensure that the central government continues to control oil revenue.

The U.S. government has policy instruments available to help in all three areas.

Prevent a Kurdish Takeover of Kirkuk

Kirkuk is not currently part of the autonomous Kurdish region, but many in Kurdistan would like it to be, in part for historical reasons (although the city has long been multiethnic), but, more importantly, because of Kirkuk's large oil fields. According to Iraq's constitution, by the end of 2007, a census and local referendum must be held to determine the status of Kirkuk. In anticipation of this, the Kurdish militias, the *peshmerga*, have taken measures to establish control of Kirkuk, encouraging Kurds to move into the area, seizing property from individuals who are not Kurds, and setting up checkpoints on access roads to verify ethnic identities. Because recent Iraqi governments have been so weak, they have found it difficult to resist these measures.

A Kurdish takeover of Kirkuk would exacerbate violence in that city and might encourage Kurds and other groups to try to take control and carry out ethnic cleansing elsewhere. It would heighten tensions with Sunnis and Shias, as well as other Iraqi ethnic groups. Most importantly, it would make it highly unlikely that a unity government would stay together, as it would be seen as a first step toward Kurdish independence. U.S. policymakers should make it clear to the Kurdish parties that the United States does not support a Kurdish takeover of the city. They should encourage efforts to reach a negotiated settlement for the future of the city, changing the constitutional provisions through the constitutional review process if necessary. The U.S. administration should notify the Kurds that, if the *peshmerga* continue to engage in ethnic cleansing, the U.S. government will support the Arab parties on the issue of Kirkuk to the point of using U.S. military forces to stop these actions. The U.S. government should be prepared to act on these threats.[1]

---

[1] The Iraq Study Group advocates postponing, until an unspecified future date, the referendum on Kirkuk's status, which the Iraqi constitution mandates be held in 2007. It also recommends that the issue of the status of Kirkuk be transferred to an international Iraqi support group for final resolution (Baker, Hamilton, and Eagleburger, 2006, p. 66).

The Kurdish parties will seek U.S. support for Kurdish aspirations or request that the United States take a hands-off approach. They will cite the history of Kurdish-U.S. friendship, continuing Kurdish support for the United States throughout the war, and the tragedies of Kurdish history. But, because the Kurds are likely to back down if they truly fear the loss of U.S. support, the United States has the capacity to influence the situation.

Oppose the Creation of New Regions

The Iraqi constitution calls for a federal state, but *federalism* is loosely defined. The constitution grants autonomy to the Kurdish region, which currently consists of three provinces (governorates). Both the constitution and legislation passed by the Iraqi parliament in October 2006 allow for the creation of additional autonomous regions if provinces voluntarily band together to do so. The legislation prevents the formation of new regions for at least 18 months, meaning that the formation of new regions could begin in spring 2008.[2]

If new regions are created, they will be drawn along sectarian lines. Because Iraq's sectarian and ethnic populations are so intermingled, no delineation can clearly separate one group from another. Kurds, Sunnis, and Shias will be left on both sides of any given boundary. The creation of additional regions would almost certainly trigger efforts to cleanse multiethnic neighborhoods through violence.

Of Iraq's 18 provinces, nine are predominantly Shiite, three predominately Kurdish, and three predominantly Sunni. The rest, including Baghdad, are mixed, but all provinces contain areas of great ethnic and sectarian diversity. Iraq's oil wealth is concentrated in the southern, Shia provinces and in the area around Kirkuk. For this reason, the Sunni community generally opposes the creation of new autonomous regions. Many Sunnis fear that new regions will leave the Sunnis with less political power and worse economic prospects, as regions with oil and the autonomy to administer their wealth will seek disproportionate shares of Iraq's oil revenues.

---

[2] Semple (2006).

The moratorium on the formation of new regions until spring 2008 buys some time, during which the U.S. government can work to discourage the creation of new regions. During this period, the U.S. government should use official U.S. policy statements and discussions with Iraqi government officials, parliamentarians, and other political leaders to underline the U.S. view that the creation of more regions would not be in Iraq's best interests.

The U.S. government has limited leverage if it uses suasion alone. U.S. assistance, however, can also be used to discourage the creation of more regions. Over the past year, some U.S. aid has been retargeted toward provinces through Provincial Reconstruction Teams (PRTs). The purpose of these teams is to provide resources and training to local politicians to build their capacity to provide government services, manage funds and projects, and improve the efficacy of assistance projects by tying them more closely to local needs. PRTs and assistance to provinces can be used to weaken initiatives to create regional governments by fostering the independence of provincial governments from proposed regional governments while strengthening and improving ties between these provinces and the central government in Baghdad. Efforts to improve government operations at the provincial level should focus on improving coordination between the central and provincial governments, thereby building institutional linkages that would make the creation of new regional governments less appealing and providing incentives for provincial officials to support continued central government control of oil revenues. Assistance should be targeted at provinces in the south that are the most likely candidates for inclusion in new regions. Key initiatives include devolving authority for public health clinics and schools while improving the transfer of funds to them from the health and education ministries, respectively. As part of this process, the United States should target its assistance programs at improving the capacity of Iraqi ministries to design programs, disburse monies, and monitor and audit results. Such an approach provides for local autonomy without threatening the role of the central government.

Because this effort will take time, it must begin as soon as possible if it is to bear fruit. By building on existing U.S. programs and focusing them on specific, long-term goals, it can create institutional arrangements that diminish the incentives to create more autonomous regions.

Keep Oil Revenues in the Hands of the Central Government

In 2005, oil exports accounted for 93 percent of the revenues of the Iraqi government; they will continue to account for more than 85 percent of planned government revenue for the foreseeable future. Without these projected revenues, the Iraqi central government will be unable to govern: It will be unable to pay security forces; fund government support programs such as the Public Distribution System (PDS), which provides food; or run clinics and schools.

Both the Kurds and those Shia groups that are pushing to set up one or more new regions seek more autonomy in part because they seek to control revenue from local oil operations. The Kurds have already sold drilling rights in the Kurdish governorates. However, geography need not necessarily determine control over oil revenues. Even if Iraq splits into regions, the key issue will be who gets the check: the new regional governments or the central government?

If new autonomous regions are created and gain control of local oil resources, the central government will be weakened financially. Regions will finance themselves, increasing their independence, and the central government will lack the funds needed to provide government services or pay for security forces. The regions will then take responsibility for providing these services and security, contributing to increased sectarianism and the potential breakup of the country. Conflicts over territory will deepen as regions seek to gain and cement control over resource-rich land.

The U.S. government should make it clear to Iraqi political leaders who desire U.S. support that the Iraqi national government must control oil revenues.[3] These policy statements should be made discreetly in bilateral meetings. The U.S. government should also use its influence to

---

[3] The Iraq Study Group argued that the federal government needs to retain control of oil revenues and that oil revenues need to be disbursed on the basis of population. The group argued that regional control of oil revenues would contribute to the disintegration of Iraq (Baker, Hamilton, and Eagleburger, 2006, p. 65).

pressure international oil companies with U.S. operations to make all payments for Iraqi oil to the Iraqi central government, not to regional governments. Exploration agreements should be signed with the Iraqi national government, not with regional governments.

As the Iraqi government debates these issues, the U.S. government should provide assistance to help it develop proposals for ensuring the equal distribution of oil revenues. Because they account for almost all government revenues, initially, oil revenues will be needed to fund Iraqi government operations at all levels—central, regional, and provincial—and to invest in infrastructure.

If oil production and revenues were to expand, the Iraqi government could provide a national oil dividend to be dispensed to all Iraqi citizens. Such a dividend would help limit the size of the Iraqi government, thereby reducing corruption. It would solidify support for a unitary state. It could also replace the current highly inefficient system of food rations and thereby provide an economic impetus to Iraqi agriculture.

Engaging Iraq's Neighbors

The United States has defined its mission in Iraq to preclude the cooperation of many regional states: The U.S. government has stated that the intervention in Iraq is a means of effecting democratization elsewhere in the Middle East, a position that many regional powers see as espousing regime change. As a result, while all of Iraq's neighbors are concerned about the slide toward civil war and none wants to see a complete failure of the U.S. mission, they also—with the possible exceptions of Jordan, Kuwait, and Turkey—do not want to see its unqualified success.

That said, there is room for progress. All of Iraq's neighbors favor a unified Iraq strong enough to maintain its territorial integrity but not so powerful as to threaten them. None favors the creation of powerful autonomous regions or the breakup of Iraq. There are, however, major disagreements among them about the ideal nature of the Iraqi state, many of which mirror the divisions within Iraq itself. Saudi Arabia and

Jordan share Sunni concerns about Shia ascendancy; Iran backs Shia claims and supports various Shia militias; and Turkey, like Iran and Syria, opposes an independent or even highly autonomous Kurdistan. Iraq's neighbors are alarmed at the violence, but, because many neighboring states support one or another of the violent parties, they have fed the violence they fear.

As long as Iraq's neighbors support violent factions in Iraq, those factions retain both the incentives and capacity to keep fighting. Thus, neighbors will need to cooperate to secure peace. Bosnia in the mid-1990s and Afghanistan after September 11, 2001, demonstrated that the cooperation of neighboring states is a crucial factor in piecing back together a broken society. Serbia's, Bosnia's, and Croatia's presidents were key participants at the discussions that led to the Dayton Accords and the resolution of the Bosnian conflict—despite their personal responsibility for precipitating and continuing the war. Pakistan, Iran, Russia, and India were key partners in creating the new government in Afghanistan, although each had supported different factions in Afghanistan. Iraq's neighbors must be similarly engaged, which requires that the U.S. government undertake direct discussions with all those governments, emphasizing sovereignty, territorial integrity, power-sharing, and stability for Iraq.[4]

Iraq's neighbors have been meeting to discuss Iraq's future, most recently in Tehran. Until March 2007, they did so largely without Iraq, the United States, or the European powers. The U.S. government should build on the initial steps taken at the March conference to help ensure that a broad group that includes itself, Iraq, the United Kingdom, Japan (which has not been involved to date), and other major powers with an interest in a stable Iraq continue to meet regularly. This group should become a basis for a regional peace process designed to stabilize Iraq and rest on principles of noninterference, the territorial integrity of Iraq, and greater regional involvement in reconciling Iraq's warring groups. A more comprehensive regional security com-

---

[4]   Engaging in multilateral and bilateral talks about the future of Iraq with all of Iraq's neighbors was a key recommendation of the Iraq Study Group (Baker, Hamilton, and Eagleburger, 2006, pp. 50–58).

pact could evolve out of this process, but it is not a prerequisite and would depend on whether a consensus is first reached on Iraq.

The U.S. government should also build on the interactions with Iran in March 2007 to develop bilateral talks with all of Iraq's neighbors, including Iran and Syria, to continuously discuss efforts to stabilize Iraq. Discussions with Syria and Iran should be frank but focused on pursuing areas in which interests are congruent rather than on differences. If Iran or Syria insists on adding other issues to the agenda, the U.S. government should, within limits, consider broader discussions (if not necessarily any demands made in those discussions). Meeting with representatives of another state should not be seen as a reward but as a standard foreign policy tool of the U.S. government. At the same time, it will remain very much in U.S. interests to monitor Iranian, Saudi, and Syrian activities in and regarding Iraq and to assess their implications for U.S. interests.

Regional initiatives, such as the Arab League's Iraq Reconciliation Program, should also be given more prominence. UN efforts in support of the government's dialogue and reconciliation program should receive more support as well.

U.S. willingness to engage all of Iraq's neighbors can make a major difference in Iraq's slide deeper into civil war. It is not a guarantee of success, but it is almost certainly a prerequisite.

CHAPTER FOUR

Security: Targeting Aid and Influence

Militias and other armed groups loyal to political or ethnic factions
represented within the government perpetrate most sectarian violence.
These groups have to be stopped from engaging in violence, reduced in
size, and eventually disbanded. Current strategies rely increasingly on
Iraq's security forces to contain violence, with the goal of their taking
primary responsibility for this mission. However, Iraq's security forces
are staffed in large part by former or current members of the very groups
they must restrain to pacify the country successfully. Despite training programs financed by assistance from the United States and other
Coalition partners, in aggregate, these forces are failing to improve
the security of Iraq's citizens. While some units, notably in the army,
are performing well, other individuals and units, notably in the police
forces, contribute to, rather than combat, sectarian and criminal violence. The proportion that is part of the problem shows no signs of
shrinking, but, rather, appears to be growing. Reversing these trends is
crucial to reducing the violence.

Get the Ministry of Interior Under Control

Ministry of Interior (MoI) officials currently operate with insufficient
oversight or control. The MoI has been accused of harboring Shia
squads that assassinate political opponents and Sunnis suspected of

supporting the insurgency.[1] Some police units have engaged in kidnapping and extortion. Such abuses have contributed to the rise of sectarian conflict and overall violence.

One important immediate change in the security forces should be in vetting and appointing officials. Senior officials throughout the Iraqi government perceive bestowing jobs on their supporters as their right. The government has exerted little control over the number of workers hired and, therefore, over payroll. Too many people are getting paid without regard to whether they work. This system has made it easy for politicians to employ partisan fighters in the MoI. Although patronage has a long tradition in Iraq and cannot be overcome quickly, better controls can make a difference. Setting minimum standards of performance and enforcing disciplinary codes would result in some improvement.

Some efforts have been made to implement reforms, including those by the current interior minister, Jawad al-Bolani, but the scale of the problem and insufficient senior political support have flummoxed efforts.[2] Some argue that the MoI is beyond repair, that it should be dismantled and rebuilt from scratch. In an environment in which an outside force could provide security, it might be possible to ensure that current MoI personnel, including police, give up their weapons and are either rehired once they have been vetted or severed from government employment and helped to find new positions outside the government. However, MoI patrols and personnel do deter some violent activity and counter some criminal activity. Without means to provide security during the transition, dismantling the MoI would likely lead to increased violence. In the absence of any police presence, today's high levels of crime would rise even higher.

Wholesale replacement of the MoI administration and bureaucratic staff would create its own set of challenges but might be feasible. A new, vetted staff would have to be available before the former staff has been dismissed—a difficult undertaking. Alternatively, the MoI could be reconstituted one department at a time. However, the antici-

---

[1] See Moore (2006a, 2006b) and Tavernise (2006).

[2] See Wong and von Zielbauer (2006).

pated changes could lead to efforts by personnel to exploit their current positions to the fullest while they are still in office.

Because of these challenges, complete dismantling of the ministry is probably infeasible. However, unless the effort to clean up the MoI receives consistent support from all parties in Iraq's government, it will remain a contributor, rather than an impediment, to violence.

The government of Iraq has committed to reform the MoI. The minister has laid out a vision for a reformed ministry, and the prime minister is considering reform proposals, for instance, surrounding restructuring the ministry and purging officials involved in abuses. The U.S. government needs to ensure that these reform efforts are carried through and extended. The key is not simply to do a "one-off" sweep that removes certain individuals but to put in place, and sustain, systemic reforms that will reduce the opportunities for abuse and corruption in the future. The U.S. government can back the following further reforms:

1. The Iraqi government should give the MoI a deadline, perhaps no more than two months, to complete the ongoing effort to compile a complete list of employees and descriptions of their jobs.[3] After this period, only people on the list would receive a salary. Those not on the list would be removed.

2. A system of biometric identification cards is being developed for the Iraqi armed forces and for the MoI.[4] This effort should be completed. Cards should not be issued until personnel lists are complete, and then only to personnel on the lists. This system will also make it possible to end access if and when persons are removed from the roster—this access policy must be rigorously enforced.

3. The Council of Ministers should create hiring boards composed of representatives from each of the major political groupings for key positions in each of the major departments of the MoI. The

---

[3] The MoI will soon have in place the IT infrastructure to capture and store these lists in the form of personnel databases.

[4] Author conversation with Coalition official, winter 2006.

boards would have to approve all new hires. Only the boards would be allowed to add individuals to the list of employees and only employees on the list would receive paychecks. In the case of the locally based Iraqi Police Service (IPS), the boards would reflect the composition of the local polities.

4. In addition to making decisions about hires, the boards would investigate all current employees to determine whether they have been involved in illegal activities or sectarian violence. The staff assigned to the boards would check for fraud by determining whether each employee actually exists and reports for work. Some investigations of this sort are under way now; they should become universal. Employees accused of illegal activities should be prosecuted and, if convicted, terminated and punished. This must include high-level officials and those close to them—otherwise, the effort will be neither credible nor effective.

5. The finance ministry, which controls payments to MoI staff and police, should shift from a system of lump-sum payments to localities to individual payments to each employee. Once electronic payment systems become available, hopefully during 2007, the finance ministry should move salary payments from cash to electronic deposits, limiting the ability of government officials to take a cut from their employees' paychecks.[5]

6. The Iraqi government should eliminate units and departments of the MoI that have been credibly accused of wide-scale corruption or infiltrated by antigovernment agents or do not serve a useful purpose. When a department or unit has been disbanded, individual staff members should be welcome to reapply for other jobs in the MoI, after they have been fully vetted.

---

[5]   The Iraq Study Group recommends that salary payment for local police be consolidated in the MoI (Baker, Hamilton, and Eagleburger, 2006, p. 80). We argue that, even if consolidated at the MoI, the ministry would still exercise too little control. In our view, the Ministry of Finance provides a more effective avenue for limiting payments of government salaries to supporters of ministers.

Individuals who lose their jobs as a result of the development of jobs lists and better vetting will have reason to be angry with Iraq's government and the Coalition. Those who are not accused of crimes and thus not subject to prosecution should be offered short-term unemployment insurance and access to training programs while they seek work or, if they are eligible, a retirement package. The MoI should ensure that police and other MoI security personnel and units that are declared redundant do not retain access to weapons or armories.

The U.S. government should support these actions through all the policy instruments at its disposal. The U.S. mission and Multi-National Force–Iraq should continue to emphasize the importance of reforming the MoI. If the reforms are not implemented, the United States should withdraw support from those parts of the Iraqi government that have failed to implement them. Aside from encouraging the reforms detailed here, the U.S. government should share with Iraqi government officials U.S. assessments of the involvement of current and proposed MoI personnel in perpetrating violence. Ongoing efforts to provide additional training to all personnel of the centrally based National Police can support the vetting effort and must be consciously used to do so. The U.S. Agency for International Development (USAID), along with Multi-National Security Transition Command–Iraq (MNSTC-I), should accelerate programs to install financial management information systems in the Iraqi government, especially in the MoI. The U.S. government should also assist the Iraqi government in creating a unified electronic employment registry and payroll system so that it can track all employees and ensure that government employees receive their full wages, without their superiors taking a cut.[6]

Although less of a problem than the MoI, the Ministry of Defense should be subject to similar reviews, oversight, and financial controls, as should the rest of the government. The security ministries should be the first priority, however.

---

[6] If wages are deposited into accounts accessible to the families of personnel, this can also help alleviate high rates of absenteeism among the security forces, as some of this is caused by deployed personnel traveling home to provide money to their families.

The United States' ability to effect these changes is not as strong as might be wished. It will be especially important to ensure that USAID and MNSTC-I have sufficient, high-quality resources to support these reforms.[7] Cleaning up the MoI is a prerequisite for creating security forces in Iraq that can be effectively used to combat violence. However, as violence continues and sectarian divides deepen, a reformed and unified MoI may become simply impossible for Iraq in the near term.

Improve Policing

Police are responsible for controlling crime, the primary source of insecurity for most Iraqis living outside of Baghdad, Diyala, or Al Anbar. If police were to successfully reduce crime throughout Iraq, they would help starve the insurgencies of weapons, funds, and support. The general atmosphere of lawlessness in Iraq makes it easier for insurgents to move, communicate, and attack U.S. and Iraqi government forces.

Police should ideally be the first line of defense against internal violence. Although they will not yet be able to operate with extensive support from the Iraqi army and Coalition forces, it is important to at least put a civil police "face" on all operations. By making suppression of Iraq's internal violence a police issue, minimizing the role of Coalition and Iraqi military forces, perceptions of violent actors as defenders of national, ethnic, or religious interests might be transformed into perceptions of them as common criminals, helping dampen nationalist and sectarian violence. Iraqi police do not face the cultural, linguistic, and (given training) professional challenges that Coalition forces face when they perform law enforcement duties in Iraq. The spur to the insurgency provided by cultural blunders perpetrated by the Coalition would be mitigated if Iraqi police were in the forefront of law enforcement. The more that Coalition military forces are involved in curfews, responses to civil unrest, and combating criminal violence, the more

---

[7] An important step, aside from financial resources, will be to recruit and retain a cadre of U.S. experts with deep knowledge of the MoI and Iraqi police rather than the current practice of rotating most personnel on an annual, or even shorter, basis.

that Iraqis feel they are under occupation. The more that military forces are involved in these actions, the more likely it is that military, rather than police, tactics will be used—potentially making Iraqis feel less rather than more secure.

The Coalition should make it a priority to have Iraqi police handle as many cases relating to violence, whatever its origin, as possible. The U.S. government should ensure that current programs to train and equip Iraqi police and internal security forces are adequately funded and are effective in improving the performance of these units. Comprehensive and frequent reviews of current efforts will be needed to achieve this goal. A commitment to long-term funding that provides the MoI and IPS some certainty over future U.S. commitments is also important.

Cleaning up the police force is even more important than training. Police units need to be purged of lawbreakers if they are to be credible and effective. The focus of assistance programs for the police is now shifting from numbers of police officers trained to their professionalization; this emphasis needs to be taken seriously and an equal focus needs to be given to incorporating accountability into the police management system. To achieve this goal, more international police officers should be embedded with local police forces, especially in Baghdad. Military police personnel, used to make up for shortfalls in civilian police, are imperfect substitutes, because military police necessarily use different tactics and have different training than civilian police do—and it is civilian policing capacity that Iraq needs. Wherever and whenever feasible, international officers should patrol with Iraqi police. But their primary task should be to mentor, train, and monitor local police commanders. Mentors should continue to report on corrupt or incompetent officers so that Coalition officials can relay this information to the Iraqi government for action.[8]

The U.S. government should provide funding to improve police leadership training courses and to ensure appropriate equipping of police forces. The Iraqi government should be encouraged to make

---

[8] The Iraq Study Group also recommends that more international police officers be embedded with Iraqi forces (Baker, Hamilton, and Eagleburger, 2006, p. 82).

superior performance in these programs mandatory for promotion while making performance on the job the most important factor. All officers should cycle through additional training programs on a regular basis.

In some cases, units of the centrally managed National Police, a heavily armed, mobile intervention force that also includes specialized functions such as emergency response and public order, have been effective in fighting crime and terrorism. These units are some of the more capable police forces in Iraq. They have also been implicated in sectarian violence; some have operated as death squads. Embedding mentors within the National Police has been helpful in uncovering and preventing malfeasance but is unlikely to be fully effective, in part because members of the Iraqi government will resist it.

An effort is currently under way to ensure that all National Police officers receive additional training. This training provides an opportunity to examine each unit and vet its personnel. We understand that an effort is now under way to adapt the training to focus more on policing than on military tactics.[9] This must be implemented and built on. The recent offer of training assistance by the Italian carabinieri is welcome in this regard. We further recommend that all National Police units should undergo comprehensive investigations. Coalition forces as well as Iraqi officials should investigate complaints. They should make results of these investigations public, and individuals should be prosecuted and otherwise held accountable for their actions. Units with records of abuse should be disbanded. As with other disbanded MoI units, individuals serving in these units who are not implicated in crimes should be able to apply for work elsewhere in the MoI, after vetting. They should not be routinely reassigned elsewhere.

In the near term, there are trade-offs between the need to reform the police, and thus rely more on Coalition and Iraqi military forces, and the need to fight violence by utilizing police units to the greatest extent possible. Vetting will reduce police ranks even as the police become central to responding to Iraq's security needs. But the alternative of maintaining an unreliable force is worse. A visible, effective

---

[9]   DoD (2006).

police presence is critical to deterring violence and changing public perceptions, but, as that is developed, the existing police will continue to rely heavily on Coalition forces and the Iraqi army for support and force protection.

Police Organization and Recruiting

Lessons from other insurgencies, such as Malaya, show that police primacy, the development of trust in the local government, and community policing are critical to successful counterinsurgency operations. They are also helpful ways to fight sectarian conflict. While national standards for training, pay, and force structure for police have their advantages, recruiting a police force nationally and deploying it without regard to the origin of the force fails to foster the levels of trust that local police recruitment and stationing can create. The deployment of Shia or Kurdish forces in Sunni areas aggravates sectarian tensions. The police are considered factions in the conflict.[10] When police are recruited from the communities in which they live, the local populace is more likely to report crimes and unusual activity. The IPS is already recruited and based locally. More oversight over IPS recruitment is needed to track and vet recruited personnel and to ensure that the ethnic mix of police in a community reflects that of the community as a whole.

The downside to local police forces is that they may include members of militias or refuse to confront local militias or insurgents. Although the IPS is locally recruited and based, the Iraqi government should have the capacity to insist that local forces operate professionally and not engage in abuses. The central government should also have the capacity to require local officials to immediately remove individuals or units not doing their jobs. If the effort to build local police forces focused on establishing law and order fails, these forces might contribute to the breakup of Iraq. However, failure to develop

---

[10] Discussions with U.S. officials and Iraqis (2005–2007). For a press account, see Wong and von Zielbauer (2006).

local policing will perpetuate violence and distrust. The exact relationships between the national and local police forces remains to be determined by the constitutional review and the finalized law on governorates, but the U.S. government should encourage Iraqi legislators to keep these principles in mind.

Law and Order

Effective policing requires courts and prisons to process those apprehended, adjudicate their cases, and punish those convicted of transgressions. Without a criminal justice system that provides the means and procedures to arrest, try, judge, and incarcerate suspects, those apprehended by the police are either jailed without due process or are released back onto the street. Overcrowded prisons filled with prisoners held without charge fuel discontent and violence, as does the automatic release of suspected criminals without trial. In short, a functioning justice system is critical if security is to be improved in Iraq.

The existing Iraqi criminal justice system does not function well. Although some parts of an effective, accountable system exist, others do not. The Coalition should make the creation of an effective justice system a priority. The U.S. government should work with the Iraqi government through mentors, monitoring, and training to ensure at least a minimal level of due process for people whom the police apprehend and proper oversight of prisons to prevent abuse. In an environment in which judges and attorneys fear for their lives, providing prosecutors and judges with bodyguards and other protection has not been as effective as hoped. The U.S. government should finance or help the Iraqi government to provide more protection for judges and prosecutors.[11]

The Iraqi government should be encouraged to move more criminal trials out of Baghdad and other violent areas to more secure regions. Not all parts of Iraq are unstable. Accused criminals can be tried in regions and areas where security is better and judges and other officers

---

[11] The Iraq Study Group has also made this recommendation to increase U.S. assistance for courts, prosecutors, and prisons (Baker, Hamilton, and Eagleburger, 2006, p. 83).

of the court could be more effectively protected. Venues would have to be changed with sensitivity to ethnic and sectarian tensions.

The courts could be improved through increased technical assistance. USAID should provide more funding to implement electronic or simplified, paper-based tracking of cases. This would help ease the strain on overburdened courts. In addition, U.S. assistance programs should prioritize the building of sufficient additional prisons and ensuring international access to all prisons to monitor conditions. The United States also needs to do a better job of incorporating the Iraqi judicial system into its security planning.[12]

Reduce Financial Flows to Militias and Other Illegal Groups

The Iraqi security forces are often unwilling to confront militias or insurgents because of ties of these groups to government officials and because members of the militias and insurgency have joined the security forces. Financial tools, however, can complement force by reducing the militias' resources.

Combatants in Iraq obtain funds from four major sources: government payrolls; the resale and smuggling of gasoline and diesel fuel; extortion, robbery, and kidnapping; and other countries. Many militia members are on government payrolls. The Kurdish regional government pays the *peshmerga* from government funds. The Iraqi government has divided up ministries by political party. Each party treats its ministries as its own fiefdoms. For example, Muqtada al-Sadr controls the health, transportation, and agriculture ministries, among others. These ministers and their deputies put militia members on the payrolls of the Facility Protection Service, police, and other parts of the government's civilian workforce. Ministers also embezzle funds from government coffers to pay their supporters.

---

[12] According to sources in Baghdad, there have been reports that the U.S. and Iraqi governments failed to expand the capacity of the Iraqi judicial and prison systems in preparation for the expected surge of detainees arising from the Baghdad security plan in spring 2007.

Smuggling and the resale of diesel fuel and gasoline is a primary source of hundreds of millions of dollars in funding for all combatants, especially Sunni insurgent groups. Extortion, kidnappings, and robberies have become an important source of funds. As in many civil conflicts, the line between criminal activity and politically inspired conflict blurs, as insurgents become impossible to differentiate from common criminals. Foreign powers, most notably Iran, also provide funding.[13]

Although the Iraqi government cannot stop the cash flow to militias and insurgents overnight, it can slow the flow, and eventually reduce it to a trickle. The government, in conformance with its stand-by agreement with the International Monetary Fund (IMF), should create a governmentwide employment registry. Only people on the registry would receive paychecks. At the same time, all payroll functions should be shifted to the Ministry of Finance. All government jobs would have to be included in the budget. Individuals could obtain a job only if the position has been designated in the budget process.

Personnel boards (like those recommended for MoI) should be set up in every ministry and composed of representatives of all ethnic, religious, and political factions in the government. The board would approve all new senior hires; approval should be unanimous. This system would permit political factions to veto senior civil servants who are known to be engaged in death squads or to otherwise act against the interests of other coalition parties.

The multifaction boards in each ministry should be given the power to investigate and turn over for prosecution those employees suspected of involvement in sectarian violence or insurgent activity. Such a procedure would make it much harder for active militia fighters and insurgents to remain on the government payroll.

The U.S. government should assist the Iraqi government in accelerating the introduction of electronic payroll systems and bank transfers by the Ministry of Finance to pay government workers. Past Iraqi

---

[13] Discussions with Iraqi citizens, government officials, U.S. government officials, U.S. government contractors, and U.S. military personnel in Baghdad, USCENTCOM, and Washington, D.C. (2004–2007).

governments had agreed to set up a system of electronic transfers by 2005. By stipulating that most government wages will have to be paid electronically and by putting payroll functions out for tender, the government would accelerate the introduction of more secure payments, stimulate the development of the banking sector, and, most importantly, reduce the diversion of payroll funds into the wrong pockets.

The U.S. government can also provide technical assistance for audit programs, financial management systems, and other financial controls. These measures will also help promote administrative procedures that increase transparency and reduce corruption. Although some officials may resist them, their very existence will make it more difficult for government personnel to evade controls.

As the Iraqi banking system gets on its feet, the U.S. government can provide assistance to ensure that foreign funders cannot freely utilize the system to transfer monies into Iraq. Anti–money-laundering techniques could go some way to reducing flows of funds from foreign sources.[14]

Coalition Force Employment

Part of the insurgency, and support for it, is driven by opposition to the U.S. presence in Iraq. Although those who most strongly oppose this presence are predominantly Sunni, some Shia, most notably members of militias tied to al-Sadr, also oppose foreign forces. Even as sectarian conflict deepens, opposition to the presence of U.S. forces will be unlikely to decline.

The more visible, competent, and loyal the Iraqi forces become, the more the Iraqi government will be viewed as legitimate. U.S. forces have been turning operations over to Iraqi security personnel as rapidly as possible, but are necessarily continuing to assist, supervise, mentor, and monitor behavior. Effectiveness and loyalty dictate the speed with which Iraqi forces can take on most tasks. To date, both have often been low. Despite the deficiencies of Iraqi forces, we recommend that

---

[14] Black market energy sales are another related issue and are discussed in the next chapter.

Coalition forces always patrol with Iraqi forces; no foreign forces should patrol without Iraqi forces.

Although training remains important, U.S. and other Coalition forces should focus on mentoring Iraqi forces, particularly commanders. Mentors should emphasize unit cohesion and loyalty. Both joint patrols and mentors serve an important oversight role as well. Even as we recommend that Coalition forces not patrol without Iraqi counterparts, we also recommend that, unless it would compromise the mission, Iraqi units patrol either jointly with Coalition personnel or accompanied by mentors.

Increasing the number of mentors can help with these and other concerns. For example, current security regulations that require that U.S. military personnel not patrol in groups smaller than nine hamper efforts to more closely monitor Iraqi forces, as they preclude the 12-person teams assigned to Iraqi battalions from splitting into smaller teams so that they can patrol with more Iraqi units. As with the police, U.S. forces should be frequently reminded of their responsibility for monitoring the behavior and competence of Iraqi personnel. Embedding and mentoring have been among the most fruitful efforts undertaken to date to improve Iraqi security forces; these efforts should be pursued even more vigorously.[15]

The joint force commander in Iraq should weigh the costs and benefits of banning air strikes in urban areas, or at least of the use of more powerful weapons. The harm to Iraqi government and security force credibility that results from collateral damage in such strikes may outweigh the benefits of destroying specific targets. The impact on civilian populations of all force use, including artillery, should be carefully considered. Rules of engagement for ground forces have been tightened already. Rules concerning the use of air power should be carefully and routinely reviewed, especially concerning the impact on the civilian population.

---

[15] For more on these issues, see DoD (2006). See also Oliker (2006).

Balance Baghdad and the Rest of Iraq

In the absence of sufficient forces to suppress violence in its many forms, commanders have sought to focus forces where they are needed most. Baghdad is home to almost a quarter of Iraq's population, the seat of government, and accounts for a disproportionate share of the Iraqi economy. It is also where most of the current violence is concentrated. If Baghdad lacks security, so does Iraq. This is why U.S. commanders have focused their efforts on Baghdad, appropriately emphasizing the use of Iraqi forces with Coalition support, rather than the use of U.S. forces, to secure the city.

Concentrating U.S. forces in Baghdad does run the risk of an increase in violence in other regions. Some of the sources of violence in Baghdad come from outside of Baghdad, and vice versa—violent actors and strategies can move from one part of the country to another. If current operations in Baghdad, including increased force size, finally begin to stabilize the city but violence surges elsewhere, the U.S. government should not move the additional forces to other regions at the expense of Baghdad force strength. Historical experience has shown that stabilization takes time, and removing the troops would likely result in a reversal of any success. If the rest of the country is to be stabilized, still more troops will be needed. This, of course, raises the question of sustainability, operational and political, but attempts to rotate force concentrations are very unlikely to work.

Public Information

Iraqi generals and officials from the MoI should take a much more prominent role in providing information to Iraqis and the broader public in the Middle East, especially concerning the security situation. The United States and other Coalition partners should take a much smaller role. More use should be made of joint press conferences; during these conferences, the Iraqi spokesperson should speak first. Although both Coalition commanders and the U.S. mission should continue to provide information to their publics at home, U.S. spokespeople should refer the news media more frequently to the Iraqi government's information providers.

U.S. public relations efforts should focus on bolstering public perceptions in Iraq and in the United States concerning the competence of the Iraqi government. Public relations in Iraq should focus on winning the "hearts and minds" of Iraqis for the Iraqi government. Providing information to citizens concerning what the government is doing and why is a crucial step to winning public support. Iraqi politicians, national and local, not U.S. officials, should be conveying these messages to the national and international media.

CHAPTER FIVE

How Economic Policies Can Help

Liberalize Refined Oil Product Prices

Smuggling and resale of gasoline and diesel sold at state-controlled prices are the largest source of money derived from corruption in Iraq. Although the Iraqi government has raised gasoline prices from a heavily subsidized price of just $0.04 per gallon a year ago to about $0.44 today, smugglers can get $3 or more per gallon by taking the gasoline across the border and selling it in Jordan or Turkey, or they can resell it on the domestic market for substantially more than this price. The total difference in value between the price at which the Iraqi government sells these products and their resale value in neighboring countries is on the order of $7 billion annually, equivalent to almost a fifth of Iraq's GDP. Reportedly, as much as one-third of these products are sold illegally. As noted previously, insurgents and militias take a cut of the profits from smuggling and resale to finance their operations. Proceeds from illegal sales of crude oil by government officials and from the resale of refined oil products also help fund insurgent and various other militia groups.[1] Meanwhile, the Iraqi government imports gasoline with government funds because so much is being smuggled outside the country.

Controlled prices result in lines to buy gas. When prices are kept too low, demand increases. When, as in Iraq, supply cannot keep up

---

[1] Discussions in Baghdad and Washington with specialists and providers of gasoline and diesel fuel to U.S. forces in Iraq (2003–2006).

with demand and lines form and cause widespread discontent as motorists sit in the hot sun for hours, waiting for gasoline and diesel fuel.

The Iraqi government can stop the illicit resale and smuggling of gasoline and diesel fuel by phasing out government price controls that keep the price of these fuels artificially low. The Iraqi finance ministry raised prices several times in 2006 with hardly a grumble from the populace. Prices are now 10 times higher than they were in the summer of 2005 but still a small fraction of the value of these products on the world market.

Much has been made of the potential political backlash from increasing refined oil product prices, but prices have already been raised a number of times since December 2005. Iraqi motorists have not protested much, because they already buy gasoline and diesel at much higher black market prices. Demonstrations around the first of the year following the first round of price increases were directed more at fuel shortages and long lines for gas than the increase in price. Repeated refined oil product price increases in the rest of 2006 took place without violence.

The U.S. government should work with the IMF to encourage the Iraqi government to continue to increase in prices for gasoline and diesel and fully liberalize refined oil product prices as soon as possible. In the interim, the U.S. government should encourage the Iraqi government to create workable regulations for private imports of refined oil products, as permitted under the recently passed law.[2]

Although price increases are never popular, a clear and transparent public education campaign can reduce public discontent. To mitigate public discontent, the Iraqi government should announce further increases well ahead of time, provide an explanation of why and where additional revenues will go, and increase the availability of fuel so that motorists can obtain one last tank of gas at the old price.

The Iraqi government could use its earnings from further increases in gasoline and diesel fuel prices to fund programs to help the poorest Iraqi citizens, programs that Prime Minister Nuri al-Maliki promised to introduce when he came to power. The government could also con-

---

[2]   Government of Iraq (2006b).

tinue to supply limited quantities of kerosene and liquid petroleum gas—the two fuels used most by the poor for heating and cooking—at controlled prices through the PDS, reducing the impact of price increases on lower-income Iraqis.

Improve the Operations of the Oil Ministry

Oil accounts for 60 to 70 percent of Iraq's GDP, and earnings from oil exports accounted for 96 percent of projected Iraqi tax revenues in the 2006 budget. In the 2006 budget, oil exports were projected to run 1.65 million barrels per day (mbd) at an average price of $46.60 per exported barrel, and oil production was projected to average 2.3 mbd, rising to 2.7 mbd in 2007.[3] However, production averaged just 2.1 mbd in 2006, and exports, 1.5 mbd. Fortunately, prices were higher than projected, making it possible for Iraq to exceed revenue targets. If production fails to rise in 2007 and 2008 or if oil prices continue to fall, the Iraqi budget will be under severe pressure. Investment and security programs would have to be cut. Economic growth would likely grind to a halt.

Recent declines in output are due more to mismanagement than to the insurgency. The relatively quiet southern fields account for four-fifths of production and virtually all exports, yet production has failed to rise in these fields. Exports and production have been constrained by poor maintenance and repair of oil export pipelines and misman-agement of the oil ports Mina al-Bakr and Khor Al-Maya, including strikes by workers and intermittent operations of terminals. Lack of storage facilities results in a reduction in pipeline operations at the end and beginning of loading operations. Because of complicated contract-ing procedures, much of the billions in investment budgeted for the oil industry went unspent in 2005 and 2006.

Improving the operations of the oil sector is crucial for improving security. Oil revenues provide the means to pay and equip the army, police, and legal system. If oil output is to increase, the Iraqi oil sector

---

[3]   Government of Iraq (2006a).

will have to be run more efficiently and more honestly. The U.S. government should encourage the Iraqi government to make a number of changes in policies that would improve the oil sector's prospects, including the following.

Increase Investment in Oil Production

In the first part of 2006, the Iraqi Ministry of Oil successfully increased oil output by bringing on line wells that had been closed and expanding output from existing wells. The ministry should continue to push up output by accelerating contracting for field work in the south, such as well workovers, improving southern pipeline and port management, and speeding efforts to install metering. The ministry should move aggressively to issue requests for proposals for contracts, be willing to pay a premium to compensate oil service companies for security risks, and provide better security for crews, including in the southern fields where there has been less violence than in the north. The Iraqi government also needs to make timely payments for services rendered. Payment arrears have discouraged companies from bidding on Iraqi projects in the past.

The U.S. government can encourage the Iraqi government to take these steps by pointing out the implications of budgetary shortfalls stemming from insufficient oil revenues and informing the Iraqi government that the United States will not plug holes in the budget with U.S. funds. The U.S. government should also direct foreign aid for the oil sector toward mentoring and improving management of production in the southern oil fields, management of the southern export pipeline system, and the operation of the oil terminals.

Restructure the Oil Ministry Along Commercial Lines

Depoliticizing the oil ministry would help improve operations. In 2005, the newly installed oil minister fired a number of competent technocrats. The best way to depoliticize the management of a state-owned oil company is to create a commercially oriented, well-managed, national oil company. The most successful state-owned oil companies are run by a chief executive officer who has operating authority and who answers to a board of directors, not to a minister. Although the government appoints the board and the oil minister often chairs the board, the board is responsible for the efficient operation of the company, not for meeting government policy goals. Iraq should reorganize its oil sector along these lines as soon as possible.

Within the new company, independent operating units should be created along operational and geographical lines: production and exploration, pipelines, refining, terminal operators, and retail outlets. The operating units should function as profit or cost centers. For example, the northern oil fields would fall under one profit center; the refinery at Baiji would fall under another. Incentives should be provided to unit managers to increase profits. Managers should be rewarded on the basis of operating profits generated by their area of responsibility. Such a shift would help solve the problem of properly metering and accounting for oil and refined products, as managers would have incentives to track production, sales, and purchases to justify bonuses.

The U.S. government can help Iraq with this transformation. Although a number of managers in the oil sector would like to exercise operational authority over their units, the accounting, control, and information systems needed to devolve authority effectively are not yet in place. U.S. assistance should focus on investing in these modern information management systems as well as mentoring Iraqi managers and providing professional training programs. The U.S. government should also provide funding to invest in controls within the oil fields, in processing facilities, and in tracking revenues. U.S. funds should be used to train personnel in procurement and budgeting as well.

The U.S. government should also encourage the Iraqi government to pass the oil law and to issue the necessary regulations to make the law operational. Contracting out more operations to companies that could quickly increase output would also help. The U.S. government can assist in the design and issuance of management contracts (with clear performance clauses) for the operations of oil ports, pipelines, and fields.[4]

---

[4] A number of studies have advocated adoption of simpler, more transparent contracting procedures in Iraq. See, for example, Open Society Institute and the United Nations Foundation (2004, p. 7).

To reduce the diversion of oil revenues into private pockets, the U.S. government should help the Iraqi government to start making all oil contracts, volumes, and prices publicly available, including posting them on the Internet. Such actions would enable all Iraqis and outside observers to track exports and export revenues. There are no compelling commercial reasons not to post this information; doing so would help greatly to reduce corruption.

Improve Oil-Sector Security

Oil production has failed to increase because expected investments failed to materialize, in part because of the security situation. Oil pipelines have repeatedly been blown up, refineries have been attacked, and insurgents have infiltrated the workforce. Because of the dangerous security situation, foreign oil service firms are reluctant to work in Iraq. Because these companies enjoy high demand for their services elsewhere, they can afford to forgo work in Iraq.

Efforts to improve security should focus on protecting crude oil processing facilities, terminals, refineries, the southern fields, the southern export oil pipelines, and the people who work in these facilities. Efforts to rely on tribes and local groups to protect pipelines have not been effective. Iraqi security forces should concentrate on patrolling and protecting the oil pipelines, with an emphasis on the south. The U.S. government should also encourage the Iraqi government to contract out pipeline security to private providers. Compensation for pipeline security personnel should be linked to how much oil traverses the pipeline, providing incentives to keep pipelines operating and intact. Payments to contractors for pipeline repair should be made on the basis of speed and quality. Iraqi forces such as expanded strategic infrastructure battalions should provide security for Iraqi oil infrastructure repair teams. Private security forces can continue to be used to protect foreign repair and oil service crews, but Iraqi commanders (with Coalition help) should be ready to provide backup support if repair crews are attacked.

Concentrate U.S. Grant Aid on the Security Sector and Improving Iraqi Government Operations

U.S. assistance should be concentrated on improving the capacity of the Iraqi government to provide basic government services, prevent the diversion of funds, and improve Iraqi security forces. Other activities, including private business development and agriculture, need to wait until the security environment improves. Priority tasks include implementing financial management information systems in all ministries, beginning with the security ministries; creating a governmentwide electronic employment register; and moving toward electronic payment of salaries and contracts.

Follow "Clear and Hold" Operations with Local Projects, Not Makework Job Programs

In addition to combating violence by providing security, successful campaigns to halt sectarian conflicts address the underlying causes of the violence, including economic grievances. However, in Iraq, the root causes of the conflict are political, sectarian, and personal, not economic. Iraqi combatants are not seeking land reform, workers' rights, or the nationalization of privately owned enterprises. They are seeking political control and, increasingly, revenge.

Some U.S. policymakers argue that, because young men have no other alternatives for employment, they join militias or the insurgency—thus proving the need for a policy of providing employment, even if short term. This argument reflects a misunderstanding of economic activity in Iraq. The supposedly high rates of unemployment—as much as 70 percent[5]—sometimes cited for Iraq are grossly exaggerated, as empirical evidence shows. Using international standards for measuring unemployment, the United Nations Development Programme's *Iraq Living Conditions Survey 2004*, assessed the Iraqi

---

[5]   IRIN (2006).

unemployment level at 10.5 percent.[6] Iraqi statistics, which employ a much more expansive definition of unemployment (a higher standard for number of hours worked per week to be considered employed and a lower standard for people seeking work, for example) than that used elsewhere in the world, show unemployment rates declining from 28.1 percent in 2003 to 26.4 percent in 2004 to 17.6 percent in 2006.[7] Baghdad, the most violent locale in Iraq, has an unemployment rate of 15.7 percent, about 2 percentage points below the national average.

Both Iraqi and U.S. policymakers conflate the absence of a monthly paycheck with employment. Most Iraqis, like most workers in the world today, do not earn a paycheck (the hundreds of thousands of Iraqi government employees are the exception). Rather, they work as farmers, traders, bakers, stonemasons, and day laborers. This work is often referred to as the *informal sector*, but it is the core of the economy in most countries. It has shown a remarkable dynamism despite Iraq's chaos, expanding since the U.S. invasion, fed in part by Iraqi government spending made possible by higher oil revenues and more liberal economic policies. Wages for day laborers, for example, have doubled in dollar terms over the past three years. As a result, household incomes are up substantially since Saddam Hussein's last years in power, as shown by the rise in ownership of electronics, appliances, and cars.

Most young men engaged in the conflict are motivated by religious beliefs, nationalism, a desire to protect family and friends, power, fear, and coercion. Payment for joining a militia or planting an improvised explosive device may provide an additional motivation but is often not the primary reason for engaging in the conflict.

Under these conditions, economic programs are less likely to have an effect on the conflict than are political compromise and improvements in security. Despite some short-term declines in violent activity, a sustained decline in violence has not followed U.S.-funded programs to create work in Sadr City, Ramadi, and other cities.

Another flawed approach, also geared to increasing employment, would be resuscitating Iraq's state-owned enterprises to increase

---

[6]   UNDP (2005, Vol. 1, p. 104).

[7]   Government of Iraq (2007).

employment. Aside from the misunderstanding of the employment situation, there are two additional reasons that this is a bad idea.

First, the relatively small numbers of people employed by state-owned enterprises outside the oil and electric power sectors have moved on to other economic activities—while continuing to collect paychecks from the government for their former employment. Though they may enjoy the money, they are not seeking to return to their old jobs: When the Coalition Provisional Authority asked the employees of the Mishraq Sulfur Company to go back on the job in 2004, some of the workers lit $40 million worth of sulfur on fire and destroyed the facility.

Second, there is little to resuscitate among the state-owned enterprises. Of the two-thirds not damaged beyond repair, perhaps half could, with proper management and incentives, produce something of value. But they would be capital intensive, i.e., employ relatively few people, and energy intensive. As power shortages continue to be one of the chief complaints of Iraqis, diverting limited power supplies from households and hospitals to Iraq's highly energy-inefficient cement plants would be neither politically popular nor economically sensible. Trying to give these enterprises a new lease on life will make Iraqis poorer without reducing the violence.

If the U.S. government wishes to expand economic opportunities for Iraqi businesses, it should intensify efforts to work with these private Iraqi companies to bid on contracts. Contracts should be awarded on the basis of simple, competitive bids. State-owned enterprises should also be free to bid, but they should receive no favors. Such a program would be far more successful at generating economic activity than pouring money into state-owned enterprises would be.

There are also some ways of providing assistance to local communities by the Iraqi government and coalition commanders that could help win support. These include

1. working with representative local groups to identify projects or services that the neighborhood most desires
2. using simple, transparent contracting procedures to take competitive bids from local entrepreneurs to provide the service or

project; the project should be awarded based on previously published criteria

3. working with the local community to ensure that the services and projects are completed as promised; final payment should be contingent on passing physical inspections.

The focus of these efforts should be on the project and the provision of a service, not on the number of bodies on payrolls. Iraq is a poor country. For that reason, funds should be used as effectively and efficiently as possible, not wasted on overstaffing projects.

Give the Iraqi Government Credit

U.S. armed forces are transitional actors in Iraq. If Iraq is to become stable, the Iraqi government will have to be perceived as being effective and legitimate. To bolster support for the Iraqi government, U.S.-funded projects should be branded with an Iraqi government imprimatur; improving the image of Coalition forces should take second place.

CHAPTER SIX

Policy Priorities If—and Only If—Violence Declines

If violence is dampened and Iraqi forces become more loyal and more effective at taking on the tasks of securing Iraq and Iraqis, the United States will face a new set of challenges and opportunities. Iraq, the United States, and the international community cannot assume that, if violence subsides, the battle has been won. As numerous other countries (Sudan, Liberia, Sierra Leone, Somalia, and Lebanon) have shown, it is easy to slip back into civil conflict. Another bout of violence in Iraq would be no less deadly than this one and would be just as difficult to end as positions harden further and sectarian divides widen.

If violence falls, the U.S. government will need to shift its resources and attention toward improving the political, security, and economic environments and institutionalizing those policies that have contributed to reducing violence. Currently, economic development programs and efforts to improve civil society would be a waste of resources because of the high level of violence. Amnesty programs and demobilization, disarmament, and reintegration (DDR) efforts will not be successful until the conflict subsides.

Politics and Security

Even if violence subsides, the U.S. and Iraqi governments will need to continue to work with Iraq's neighbors to ensure that Iraq becomes more stable. A stable Iraq is in the interest of all of Iraq's neighbors, although different states and interest groups have differing perspectives on what sort of stable outcome would suit them. The U.S. government will also need to continue to support a government of national unity and continue to help mentor and monitor Iraqi security forces until they can provide security on their own.

U.S.-Iraq Relations

Currently, the presence of tens of thousands of U.S. and other Coalition forces in Iraq serves, among other things, as a guarantee against external attack. When troop levels drop, the U.S. commitment to Iraq's territorial integrity will be less obvious.

The U.S. commitment can be clarified through formal agreements and arrangements between the two countries. If carefully designed, those arrangements can help bolster the Iraqi government and chances for continued peace. Iraq will remain weak for the foreseeable future. It will require continued international political and military support. If security improves as a result of U.S. policies and presence, Iraq's government will continue to see the United States as the primary guarantor of its own security and territorial integrity.

A stabilized Iraq may seek a bilateral commitment. If it does, the United States should be prepared to grant one. An explicit U.S. commitment to protect the territorial integrity of a stabilized Iraq would deter foreign meddling and domestic enemies. It would also give Iraq the liberty to avoid building up its own forces in ways that could threaten its neighbors—thereby reassuring them that it has no hostile intentions.

The U.S. government may be unwilling to provide a formal security guarantee. Since the end of the Cold War, it has preferred not to provide formal bilateral security guarantees. From the Iraqi perspective, a formal bilateral security agreement might invoke reminders of arrangements from its colonial past. Such an agreement might be subject to review and possibly ratification by the U.S. Senate, certainly if it is made in the form of a treaty. Any arrangements the United States negotiates with Iraq must be commensurate with its existing treaty commitments to Turkey and its security guarantees to Saudi Arabia, Kuwait, and other Persian Gulf states. On the other hand, there are advantages to codifying mutual commitments, especially if they improve transparency and facilitate healthy debate among Iraqis.

If the U.S. government is unwilling to provide a formal security guarantee, other arrangements and assurances would help provide external security. A UN umbrella could also be extended over future U.S.-Iraqi military arrangements, reducing both internal and regional risks. The United States and the United Nations will have to negotiate with the Iraqi government a follow-on to United Nations Security Council Resolution 1723, which expires December 31, 2007. Such a follow-on resolution should contain a clear Iraqi request for assistance from multinational forces. This arrangement could be bolstered by an explicit U.S. commitment to protect the territorial integrity of Iraq for a fixed period.

If the United States remains engaged militarily, it will require some form of security relationship to govern the continued presence of its forces on Iraqi soil, including their legal status. At present, a combination of UN resolutions and government statements govern the presence of foreign forces in Iraq. Such arrangements call into question the sovereignty of the Iraqi government, by both its people and others, especially in the Middle East. To be effective, formal arrangements would have to strike a balance between protecting U.S. personnel and avoiding the appearance of privilege for U.S. forces compared to Iraq's own security personnel and citizens. An agreement that codifies the status of U.S. personnel would have to be in clear accordance with Iraqi law.

Continued Security Assistance

Even with much improved security, Iraq will need foreign security assistance. An Iraq that is friendly with the United States will seek assistance; the United States should provide it. Training is only one component; mentoring and oversight will likely be needed for many years. In light of budgetary pressures, Iraq will have difficulty purchasing, operating, and maintaining sophisticated military equipment. Under the best of circumstances, the country will need to rely on an outside power, presumably the United States, for a variety of capabilities, including air power. The Iraqi government has more pressing needs than to invest heavily in expensive military equipment at this time. Moreover, the development of a significant offensive capability on the part of Iraq could destabilize regional security. The U.S. government should discourage the Iraqi government from investing in expensive, modern weapons and capabilities that neighbors will perceive as offensive. The United States should, however seek to establish a long-term relationship with the Iraqi armed forces as their primary source of equipment and training.

Offer Broad Amnesty

Amnesties for combatants of all stripes are often an important part of the end of hostilities. A number of negotiated agreements to end conflicts have included amnesty provisions, including the Dayton Accords for Bosnia and Herzegovina, the Esquipulas II arrangements in Central America, the Agreement for a Firm and Lasting Peace in Guatemala, Colombia's Justice and Peace Law, the Erdut Agreement for Eastern Slavonia, and the Lome Agreement in Sierra Leone.[1] In most cases, amnesty agreements are part and parcel of DDR. They guarantee former combatants freedom from prosecution if they turn in their weapons, demobilize, and rejoin society. In some cases, amnesties require full confessions of crimes committed to facilitate truth and reconciliation efforts and for the historic record. Adjudication and reparations are sometimes part of the process.

Amnesties do not always cover all combatants. Negotiators have, at times, chosen to exclude those guilty of torture, genocide, and other violations of international law. In other cases, blanket amnesties extend to all those who engaged in conflict.

Amnesties are not always successful. Unless the peace process is well advanced, amnesties tend to do little good on their own, as successive efforts in Colombia and Sierra Leone have shown. They are most effective when paired with an international peace enforcement presence, as well as a comprehensive DDR program.

In Iraq, an amnesty program will be necessary to ensure that combatants turn in their weapons and stop fighting. Such a program will

---

[1]   UN (1995), Costa Rica et al. (1995), Guatemala and Unidad Revolucionaria Nacional Guatemalteca (1998), Casa de Nariño (2006), U.S. Institute of Peace (1995), Government of Sierra Leone and Revolutionary United Front of Sierra Leone (1999).

have to be broad, encompassing insurgents who have attacked Iraqi and Coalition military personnel, though not criminals who have been tried and convicted. Whether those implicated in attacks on civilians can or ought to be given amnesty is a question for the Iraqi government, as is the decision of whether to hold trials and require or pay reparations. In principle, the broader the amnesty, the broader the peace process and the capacity to build a truly unified Iraq.

An amnesty program should not be implemented until violence abates. As numerous cases around the world have shown, amnesty will be unsuccessful if it is attempted while fighting continues.

Demobilization, Disarmament, and Reintegration

DDR of former fighters will be necessary if peace is to last, but it cannot be successfully undertaken until fighting subsides. If DDR is undertaken too soon, individuals will feign participation while continuing to fight. Efforts to undertake such a program in areas where fighting is lighter would also not be effective and would waste resources, as those groups that exist in those areas are also hedging against greater violence in the future.

If violence begins to subside, the U.S. government should help the Iraqi government to design a DDR program for such time as the fighting stops. Such a program should target members of militias, insurgents, and government security personnel who would become redundant in peacetime. The program should offer job training and other assistance to these individuals. The U.S. government should help the Iraqi government develop means of determining who was and who was not a combatant. An effort this comprehensive will be expensive. If conditions become ripe, the United States can help set up such a program by providing advice and resources and by mobilizing international support.

Intelligence

The Iraqi National Intelligence Service (INIS) does not now play an important role in providing senior Iraqi decisionmakers with intelligence that has been professionally evaluated and analyzed or in overseeing Iraqi intelligence efforts as a whole. The interior and defense ministries have their own intelligence capabilities—in the case of the MoI, several. The Ministry of State for National Security is playing a growing role in gathering and acting on intelligence. The militias, various other government agencies, and political groups also have their own sources.

While violence remains high, Coalition and Iraqi officials should focus on limiting abuses by the existing intelligence services and helping the Iraqi government sort good, accurate information from bad. In pursuit of the first goal, the U.S. government should highlight abuses for Iraqi officials and push to end them.

If violence is dampened, attention can turn to reforming intelligence operations and creating intelligence services that would serve Iraq's needs. The INIS's formal charter and legal description are for an organization that meets those criteria. It should be helped to become what it should be. Intelligence services operating under various ministries must be limited to intelligence functions commensurate with their agencies' legitimate needs. The Iraqi government will need to make a concerted effort to identify, prosecute, and disband militia and independent intelligence operations. U.S. and other Coalition advisors can provide technical assistance to develop civilian oversight over activities by intelligence services and over budgets and expenditures.

Economic Policies

U.S. economic policy leverage has diminished over the past three years. The numbers and roles of U.S.-funded senior advisors to Iraqi ministries have declined; the Iraqi government has become increasingly independent in terms of economic policy. All of the Iraq Relief and Reconstruction Fund monies have been obligated; most have been spent. Withholding aid is becoming a threat of declining value.

Despite this decline in the strength of U.S. economic policy levers, if security improves, the next few years may provide more room for U.S. policy leverage on Iraqi economic policies than the past few years have. In a more secure environment, the current government will be forced to confront the backlog of economic policy decisions ranging from refined oil product price liberalization to reforming the food ration system that has been left from the past. If the level of violence declines, the Iraqi government may well be receptive to economic policy advice even as U.S. policy leverage appears to be in decline.

Improve the Operations of the Electric Power Ministry

Long, frequent blackouts engender some of the harshest criticism from Iraqis of their government. Despite all the investment that has been poured into the electrical power sector, power is still frequently unavailable, especially in Baghdad. Yet Iraq now generates more power per capita than do countries such as Tunisia, which has twice the per capita income and a larger industrial sector.[2]

The key problems in the electric power sector, as in the oil sector, are that consumers face no incentives to limit demand and that managers and employees have few incentives to improve service. Until the sector is run on a commercial basis and consumers are billed and pay cost-recovery prices for power, Iraq will continue to be subject to frequent blackouts, regardless of the money spent on the sector.

The electric power sector needs to be restructured along lines we recommend for the oil ministry: Generating plants, the high-voltage transmission system, and regional distribution systems need to be treated as profit centers. Managers should be rewarded for maximizing profits or controlling costs. Because the ministry is neither currently charging cost-recovery prices for power nor collecting payments, the sector will need to invest in recreating a billing and collection system. A regulatory authority needs to be created to set rates that cover costs. The authority will also need to help set prices for fuels that better reflect the value of those fuels. These steps are necessary to solve the problem of excess demand and the consequent blackouts and power shortages.

If violence subsides, the U.S. government can provide assistance to the Ministry of Electric Power so that it can accelerate programs to charge, bill, and collect payments for electric power. The recent refined

---

[2]   CIA (2007) and calculated from data on electric power generation from U.S. Department of State (2005–2007, various weeks).

oil product price increases provide an opening in this regard, as Iraqis have received a signal that product subsidies will be reduced.

Improve Iraqi Welfare Programs

The Iraqi government operates a number of programs to improve living standards. None of these programs works well. The PDS provides food, soap, and other basics for free to all Iraqi households. The quality of the commodities is poor and delivery erratic. In many parts of the country, recipients sell their rations for pennies on the dollar to raise cash for other purchases. The program deprives Iraqi farmers of a large share of their potential market, as families obtain food for free rather than purchasing it from local farmers. Agricultural subsidies distort production.

Outside of education, health care, and security, welfare programs are the primary link between the Iraqi government and the populace. If Iraqis felt better served by these programs, popular support for the state would rise. The Iraqi government has been exploring alternative social welfare programs. Prime Minister al-Maliki has announced that the government is going to spend $2 billion on targeted assistance in the future, but policy proposals are just being formulated.[3] The government has been experimenting with providing cash payment in lieu of food rations. This could be increased to help compensate households for increased fuel prices. It is also attempting to target assistance to poorer households, although targeting runs the danger of creating opportunities for government bureaucrats to demand bribes in exchange for enrollment in assistance programs.

If security improves, the U.S. government should provide more technical assistance to the Iraqi government to explore and develop alternatives to the PDS for food and other subsidy programs. This assistance may be best channeled through the World Bank, which has already been working with the Iraqi government on these issues. Programs such as cash payments in lieu of supplies of food could increase allegiance to the national government.

---

[3] "Prime Minister Maliki Speech to Parliament" (2006).

End the Use of U.S. Grant Aid for Infrastructure Projects

Even if security improves, the U.S. government should provide no additional grants to pay for increased oil production or improvements to refineries. Oil prices are so high and Iraqi oil resources so rich that this sector should be able to attract commercial funding or be self-financing.

The U.S. government should also not provide further grant aid to construct infrastructure in Iraq. Further investments in water systems, electric power, roads, and other infrastructure should be funded through project financing, not grant aid. Shifting from grant aid to project lending will focus Iraqi efforts, as the government and utilities will have to present credible plans and measures to convince lenders that loans will be repaid. If investments are made wisely, the industry will generate the revenues needed to repay these loans and make additional investments. As most assistance from other countries and international financial institutions offered to Iraq is available in the form of loans, a shift to project financing will facilitate the efforts of the Iraqi government to tap these sources of aid.

CHAPTER SEVEN

Next Steps If Violence Fails to Decline

When Is It Time to Go Home?

In light of the history of violence in Iraq, efforts to stabilize the country may fail. But, because of the combat superiority of U.S. troops over Iraqi militias and insurgents, U.S. troops could probably remain in Iraq indefinitely, even if internecine conflict were to intensify. How will U.S. policymakers be able to judge when further efforts will be to no avail?

There is one true measure of success: If the number of Iraqis who die violently declines sharply, violence has abated. If the number of Iraqis who die violently fails to decline, policies are failing.

The U.S. commitment to Iraq should not be open-ended. If U.S. forces cannot reduce the violence in Iraq, their continued presence and the further expenditure of U.S. treasure and lives will prove unsustainable, even if their presence is achieving other objectives. It is clear that current levels and approaches have not succeeded. The modest surge in U.S. forces under way, if coupled with the adoption of more effective policies, might yield results. However, as higher troop levels will further strain the U.S. military, and since a great deal of time has already been given to this enterprise, we do not believe that it will take very long to see whether the effort is turning things around. If the number of Iraqis who die violently does not fall substantially by the summer of 2007, domestic political pressure to withdraw U.S. forces may become impossible to resist.

How Should We Leave?

If violence cannot be reduced, a rapid drawdown of U.S. forces may be unavoidable. Reducing or eliminating U.S. forces in Iraq will also reduce U.S. influence. As the United States draws down, the sectarian groups that are responsible for the current killings, as well as insurgents, will dictate the course of the conflict even more. Levels of violence will likely rise, as sectarian militias become unconstrained by U.S. presence. Some analysts hope that a reduction in the U.S. presence would focus Iraqi efforts, resulting in a fall in violence, as Iraqi security personnel shoulder more responsibility and militias stand back from the brink. We believe that this outcome is highly unlikely. Others argue that the militias would fight themselves to exhaustion within a short period. We note that a number of internecine conflicts have lasted decades; some have ended only when one of the parties has been completely defeated.

A total withdrawal from Iraq or even a dramatic reduction of the U.S. presence would not be a simple procedure. Withdrawals are phased and take time, and the United States will have a number of options for how to structure the withdrawal.

Some analysts have suggested that U.S. forces should retreat to the northern, Kurd-dominated provinces, from which they might deploy into other parts of Iraq as needed. Such an approach is fraught with difficulties. It would lend credence, both among Kurds and other Iraqis, to a potentially separate Kurdish state, spurring more ethnic cleansing and conflict in areas where populations are intermingled. It is also unlikely to be particularly effective against violence outside of the Kurdish areas. Once U.S. forces have been withdrawn from these other areas, the benefits of cooperation and coordination with Iraqi forces would be gone. If U.S. forces were to act in other parts of Iraq from bases in the Kurdish north, they would likely act alone and be perceived as invaders, damaging the credibility of any Iraqi government that would call for or condone such actions—and further damaging Kurdish relations with the rest of Iraq.

Another option would be to maintain a small cadre of U.S. forces as trainers and to continue to provide capabilities to the Iraqi armed forces that they currently lack, such as air power. This presumes that the withdrawal is undertaken under conditions in which Iraqi government security forces are functioning effectively, and relations between the Iraqi government and the United States remain good, despite the continued violence. Under this scenario, U.S. forces would still be concerned about force protection and clearly defining their mission. If conditions do allow such a presence, it may be worthwhile to continue to provide funds and resources to improve the capacity of the Iraqi security forces, the Ministries of Interior and Defense, and other security agencies, even after the bulk of U.S. forces have left. That said, in a violent environment, without large numbers of effective security forces (U.S. or Iraqi) meaningful training may not be tenable.

Some argue that the United States should maintain forces in Baghdad to protect Iraq's government, should one exist, even if forces have been withdrawn from the rest of Iraq. Such a presence could probably be sustained, but to little effect. U.S. forces would lack the capacity to help the Iraqi government gain control over the rest of the country. They would remain a target and likely continue to suffer casualties, and an Iraqi government protected by foreign forces might be even less effective than one eschewing such protection.

What Would Be the Repercussions of Withdrawal?

The U.S. government cannot wait until withdrawal is imminent to plan for the repercussions of leaving Iraq. It needs to start developing responses to a continuing and expanding conflict following a retreat from Iraq.

Iraq's factions would almost certainly continue to fight among themselves for control after U.S. and other coalition forces left. The unity government might or might not survive in some form but would likely lose more and more control as time goes on. Security forces would likely break into units according to political factions. Ethnic cleansing and violence would continue and might reach the level of attempted genocide. Iraq's neighbors would likely become increasingly engaged in supporting allied factions in Iraq and in trying to prevent the conflict from spilling across their borders. Iran would continue to support Shia militias. Saudi Arabia would likely support Sunni groups. Turkey might occupy a region of Iraq along its border to prevent Kurdish insurgents from crossing its border. All of Iraq's neighbors would attempt to close their borders to refugees and insurgents. These responses might well lead to an escalation of violence. Under the worst-case scenario, violence in Iraq would spread to neighboring countries—not only those that have sought to influence events in Iraq, but also Jordan and Kuwait, countries that have sought to stay out of the conflict. Refugee flows into those countries could be substantial and precipitate cross-border conflicts.

Groups such as al Qaeda in Iraq would likely continue some level of operations, but some of the impetus drawing foreign fighters to Iraq to test themselves against Coalition forces may diminish, even as other foreign troops come in to take sides in the conflict. Whether Iraq became a safe haven for terrorists would depend on what conditions it could offer terrorist groups. If al Qaeda in Iraq were able to gain control over Al Anbar province, that region could become a site for training camps and planning networks. In areas where violence continued at high levels, however, the environment might not be as conducive for such groups, which may benefit from a certain (not too high, but also not too low) level of stability to support the logistical needs of their headquarter operations.[1]

What Could the United States Do to Mitigate the Repercussions of Withdrawal?

Withdrawing from Iraq would not be the first time that a major power has left a country that it has failed to control. Postcolonial history is

---

[1]   For example, prior to Operation Enduring Freedom, al Qaeda headquartered in relatively stable, Taliban-controlled parts of Afghanistan. While absolute security is not essential, such groups are likely to seek environments in which they can function effectively, with transportation and communication capacity, so some stability is desired. For a discussion of environmental factors in an insurgency, see O'Neill (1990, pp. 53–69). Although O'Neill does not discuss stability directly, his discussion of logistical requirements raises related questions.

replete with similar instances. France left Algeria and Vietnam; Portugal left Angola and Mozambique.

This said, a U.S. withdrawal is likely to call U.S. credibility into question. It would give Iran, Syria, and Islamic terrorist groups opposed to the West a sense of victory. The civil war in Iraq would continue and could escalate after U.S. forces leave, potentially spilling over into neighboring countries. Efforts to foster reform and development in the Middle East might suffer. To mitigate these consequences, we recommend the following.

Withdraw Without Haste

Withdrawal should be announced only after first consulting with the Iraqi government and U.S. allies, especially the United Kingdom, and informing the Iraqi public and Iraq's neighbors, including countries such as Syria and Iran that consider the United States their enemy. Withdrawal should be conducted in an orderly fashion, with no sense of haste. If U.S. forces are harassed, they should strike back hard as a warning to insurgent forces. Facilities should be turned over to Iraqi forces; they should not be left empty, an invitation to looters.

Reassure Friends and Allies

The U.S. Department of State should engage in a global effort to explain why the decision to withdraw has been made, that the United States has not abandoned its commitments to other countries and allies, and that the United States will continue to defend its interests actively around the globe. The U.S. government should make it clear that it is not planning to vacate bases in the Persian Gulf or changing military commitments to other states in the region. The U.S. government should also make it clear that it will assist countries, such as Jordan, as they respond to spillovers from conflict in Iraq. During this process, the U.S. government should also discuss with the governments of Syria and Iran its reasons for withdrawal, its concerns, and its willingness to still respond militarily if other U.S. interests in the region are challenged.

Work with the United Nations to Pass a Resolution Recognizing the Territorial Integrity of Iraq

None of Iraq's neighbors has expressed an interest in dismembering the country. However, if the civil conflict intensifies, many of its neighbors might consider occupying territory temporarily or even permanently to prevent a spillover from the conflict. The U.S. government should work with Iraq's neighbors and the United Nations to pass a resolution reaffirming Iraq's territorial integrity. Commitments from Iraq's neighbors and the resolution might help forestall grabs for territory. At a minimum, international resolutions and warnings from neighbors and outside powers should make countries that might attempt to seize territory think twice about the consequences.

Help Refugees

If the conflict worsens as U.S. forces withdraw, many more Iraqis will flee the country. Jordan, Syria, Turkey, Egypt, Lebanon, and even Iran are the most likely immediate stops, although Europe, the Persian Gulf states, and the United States would also be likely choices for final destinations. The U.S. government should work with Iraq's neighbors, most notably Jordan, Syria, Egypt, Lebanon, and Turkey, to help provide funds for feeding and caring for refugees and set up centers for processing refugees for relocation to a final destination or to return home. U.S. government employees would need to be deployed to process requests for relocation to the United States and for asylum.

The U.S. government has a special obligation to take care of Iraqis who have worked for or helped the United States and have reason to fear retaliation. In the past, most notably following the fall of South Vietnam, some people who had worked for U.S. agencies and supported U.S. efforts suffered greatly following withdrawal. In the event of withdrawal, the U.S. government should set up programs to assist these Iraqis either in emigrating to the United States or in finding another safe place to live. The United States should set up processing centers to make decisions quickly and fairly. Criteria for asylum should be widely publicized. In general, they should be broad; Iraqis should be rejected only if they can provide no evidence of having assisted the United States or if investigations reveal that they pose a threat to U.S. security.

Such a policy could well result in hundreds of thousands of Iraqi refugees seeking asylum in the United States. In this event, the process of investigating claims will be time consuming. The U.S. government will need to work with the states, nonprofit organizations, churches, mosques, and other entities to provide the resources and programs needed to relocate Iraqi refugees to the United States and integrate them into U.S. society. It will also need to help and assist neighboring countries which may host refugees who are seeking asylum and to work with Middle Eastern, European, and other countries that may also be willing to provide homes to Iraqi political refugees.

Do Not Get Excited About Oil

Some analysts have suggested that the United States not withdraw from Iraq completely but maintain a secure zone around the southern oil fields, pipelines, and oil export terminals to ensure that Iraqi oil makes it to the world market. Such a policy is unnecessary and would be counterproductive. Any Iraqi group that controls the oil fields will attempt to increase production and exports to finance its operations. Oil output would cease only if the fields or terminals became fields of conflict. If Iraqi oil exports were to be cut off for an extended period, the cutoff would not necessarily result in a dramatic increase in world market oil prices. Iraq is currently an important, but not a very large, exporter. In October 2006, it exported 1.6 mbd, less than 2 percent of global consumption. In the past, when Iraq was a bigger exporter and the global supply was smaller, cutoffs in Iraqi exports did not lead to catastrophic price hikes. For example, after 1980, oil prices fell even though Iran successfully throttled most Iraqi exports of oil.

Maintain Appropriate Relations with the Successor Regime

Even if the current Iraqi government collapses in the violence, a new government or governments will eventually emerge. Despite its (or their) complexion and the views of its (or their) leaders concerning the United States, the U.S. government should engage with the new government or governments. Once it or they have begun to solidify, the U.S. government should approach leaders cautiously and, if diplomatic relations have been broken, restore them. In some instances, the U.S. government may wish to provide assistance. In almost no instance would it make sense for the U.S. government to refuse to establish diplomatic relations. The U.S. government should not let the past dictate initiatives to engage Iraq diplomatically, but should be prepared to deal with the new government on its own terms. This could mean poor relations, as might be likely to evolve with regimes dominated by those hostile to the United States. If this is the case, however, it should not be the United States that refuses to engage. As was learned during the Cold War, engagement, even with a regime hostile to U.S. interests, can help to advance those interests.

References

Baker, James Addison, Lee Hamilton, and Lawrence S. Eagleburger, *The Iraq Study Group Report*, New York: Vintage Books, 2006. As of May 7, 2007: http://www.usip.org/isg/iraq_study_group_report/report/1206/index.html

Bartholet, Jeffrey, "Sword of the Shia," *Newsweek*, December 4, 2006, p. 26.

Basu, Moni, "Iraqi Kurds, Arabs Reap a Bitter Harvest," *Atlanta Journal and Constitution*, May 29, 2003.

"Between Staying and Going: Iraq," *The Economist*, October 21, 2006.

Biden, Joseph R., Jr., and Leslie H. Gelb, "Unity Through Autonomy in Iraq," *The New York Times*, May 1, 2006, p. A19.

Brookings Institution, "Iraq Index: Tracking Reconstruction and Security in Post-Saddam Iraq," undated Web page. As of January 18, 2007: http://www.brookings.edu/iraqindex

Byman, Daniel L., and Kenneth M. Pollack, "What Next?" *The Washington Post*, August 20, 2006.

Cambanis, Thanassis, "Fractured Iraq Sees a Sunni Call to Arms," *Boston Globe*, March 27, 2005.

Casa de Nariño, Presidencia de la República de Colombia, "Gobierno Reglamento Ley de 'Justicia y Paz,'" press release, Bogotá, January 2, 2006.

Castaneda, Antonio, "Iraqi Army Struggles to Lure Sunni Arabs," Associated Press, July 14, 2006.

CIA—*see* U.S. Central Intelligence Agency.

Clover, Charles, "Ethnic Tensions Flare in Postwar Kirkuk: Clashes Between Arabs and Kurds May Be the Legacy of Ba'ath Party 'Arabisation' of the City," *Financial Times*, May 21, 2003, p. 12.

Cordesman, Anthony H., and Emma Davies, *Iraq's Sectarian and Ethnic Violence and the Evolving Insurgency: Developments Through Late January 2007*, Washington, D.C.: Center for Strategic and International Studies, January 26, 2007. As of April 12, 2007:
http://www.csis.org/media/csis/pubs/070126%5Finsurgency%5Fupdate.pdf

Costa Rica, El Salvador, Guatemala, Honduras, Nicaragua, and Panama, *Draft Resolution*, New York: United Nations, A/50/L.17, 1995.

Davis, Lynn E., J. Michael Polich, William M. Hix, Michael D. Greenberg, Stephen D. Brady, and Ronald E. Sortor, *Stretched Thin: Army Forces for Sustained Operations*, Santa Monica, Calif.: RAND Corporation, MG-362-A, 2005. As of April 12, 2007:
http://www.rand.org/pubs/monographs/MG362/

Dobbins, James, Seth G. Jones, Keith Crane, Andrew Rathmell, Brett Steele, Richard Teltschik, and Anga Timilsina, *The UN's Role in Nation-Building: From the Congo to Iraq*, Santa Monica, Calif.: RAND Corporation, MG-304-RC, 2005. As of May 22, 2007:
http://www.rand.org/pubs/monographs/MG304/

Dobbins, James, John G. McGinn, Keith Crane, Seth G. Jones, Rollie Lal, Andrew Rathmell, Rachel Swanger, and Anga Timilsina, *America's Role in Nation-Building: From Germany to Iraq*, Santa Monica, Calif.: RAND Corporation, MR-1753-RC, 2003. As of April 12, 2007:
http://www.rand.org/pubs/monograph_reports/MR1753/

DoD—*see* U.S. Department of Defense.

Enders, David, "Letter from Baghdad: The Growing Sectarian Divide," *The Nation*, April 8, 2006. As of April 12, 2007:
http://www.thenation.com/doc/20060424/enders

Filkins, Dexter, Mona Mahmood, and Khalid al-Ansary, "Kurdish and Shiite Units of Iraqi Army Clash," *The New York Times*, May 14, 2006, p. A12.

Government of Iraq, "Budget of Iraq for 2006," Baghdad, 2006a.

———, Law on Oil Products Import and Sale, Iraqi Civil Code, Baghdad, September 2006b.

———, "Employment Survey," Central Office of Statistics, Information, and Technology, Baghdad, 2007.

Government of Sierra Leone, and Revolutionary United Front of Sierra Leone, "Peace Agreement Between the Government of Sierra Leone and the Revolutionary United Front of Sierra Leone," Lomé, June 3, 1999.

Guatemala, and Unidad Revolucionaria Nacional Guatemalteca, *The Guatemala Peace Agreements*, New York: Department of Public Information, United Nations, 1998.

Hernandez, Nelson, "Iraqis Begin Duty with Refusal; Some Sunni Soldiers Say They Won't Serve Outside Home Areas," *The Washington Post*, May 2, 2006, p. A13.

Hoffman, Bruce, *Insurgency and Counterinsurgency in Iraq*, Santa Monica, Calif.: RAND Corporation, OP-127-IPC/CMEPP, 2004. As of May 22, 2007:
http://www.rand.org/pubs/occasional_papers/OP127/

Independent Electoral Commission of Iraq, undated homepage. As of January 18, 2007:
http://www.ieciraq.org/English/Frameset_english.htm

Integrated Regional Information Networks, "Iraq: Unemployment and Violence Increase Poverty," October 17, 2006. As of May 22, 2007:
http://www.irinnews.org/Report.aspx?ReportId=61892

International Crisis Group, *Iraq's Kurds: Toward an Historic Compromise?* Amman and Brussels: International Crisis Group, Middle East Report No. 26, April 8, 2004.

———, *The Next Iraqi War? Sectarianism and Civil Conflict*, Baghdad and Brussels: International Crisis Group, Middle East Report No. 52, February 27, 2006a. As of April 12, 2007:
http://www.crisisgroup.org/library/documents/middle%5Feast%5F%5F%5Fnorth%5Fafrica/iraq%5Firan%5Fgulf/52%5Fthe%5Fnext%5Firaqi%5Fwar%5Fsectarianism%5Fand%5Fcivil%5Fconflict.pdf

———, *Iraq and the Kurds: The Brewing Battle Over Kirkuk*, Amman and Brussels: International Crisis Group, Middle East Report No. 56, July 18, 2006b. As of April 12, 2007:
http://www.crisisgroup.org/library/documents/middle_east___north_africa/iraq_iran_gulf/56_iraq_and_the_kurds___the_brewing_battle_over_kirkuk.pdf

———, *After Baker-Hamilton: What to Do in Iraq*, Baghdad, Amman, Damascus, and Brussels: International Crisis Group, Middle East Report No. 60, December 19, 2006c. As of April 12, 2007:
http://www.crisisgroup.org/library/documents/middle_east___north_africa/60_after_baker_hamilton___what_to_do_in_iraq.pdf

International Republican Institute, *Survey of Iraqi Public Opinion*, June 14–June 24, 2006. As of April 12, 2007:
http://www.iri.org/mena/iraq/2006-07-19-IraqPoll.asp

Iraq Body Count, undated homepage. As of January 19, 2007:
http://www.iraqbodycount.net

IRIN—*see* Integrated Regional Information Networks.

Jervis, Rick, "'All-Time High' in Baghdad Violence: Sectarian Killings More Than Triple," *USA Today*, October 12, 2006, p. A1.

Klein, Philip, "America, Don't Leave Us," *The American Spectator Online*, September 23, 2006. As of April 27, 2007:
http://www.spectator.org/dsp_article.asp?art_id=10389

Krauthammer, Charles, "Iraq: A Civil War We Can Still Win," *The Washington Post*, September 8, 2006, p. A17.

Marr, Phebe, "Who Are Iraq's New Leaders? What Do They Want?" U.S. Institute of Peace, special report 160, Washington, D.C., March 2006. As of April 12, 2007:
http://www.usip.org/pubs/specialreports/sr160.html

Merriam-Webster, "Civil War," undated Web page. As of April 12, 2007:
http://www.m-w.com/dictionary/civil%20war

Moore, Solomon, "Police Abuses in Iraq Detailed," *Los Angeles Times*, July 9, 2006a, p. A1.

———, "The Conflict in Iraq, Killings by Shiite Militias Detailed," *The New York Times*, September 28, 2006b.

Office of the Special Inspector General for Iraq Reconstruction, *Quarterly Report to Congress*, Arlington, Va.: Office of the Inspector General, Coalition Provisional Authority, 2007. As of April 12, 2007:
http://purl.access.gpo.gov/GPO/LPS63510

Oliker, Olga, "No Law and No Order," *Parliamentary Brief*, December 1, 2006, pp. 1–3. As of April 13, 2007:
http://www.rand.org/commentary/120106PB.html

O'Neill, Bard E., *Insurgency and Terrorism: Inside Modern Revolutionary Warfare*, Washington, D.C.: Brassey's, 1990.

Open Society Institute, and the United Nations Foundation, *Iraq in Transition: Post-Conflict Challenges and Opportunities*, Washington, D.C., November 2004. As of April 13, 2007:
http://www.unfoundation.org/files/pdf/2004/iraq_Transition.pdf

Pfeiffer, Eric, "Troops to Remainin [sic] Iraq, Bush Says," *The Washington Times*, October 23, 2006, p. A1.

Poole, Oliver, "Sectarian Violence Grips Baghdad," *The Daily Telegraph* (London), September 10, 2005.

"Prime Minister Maliki Speech to Parliament," *Al-Iraqiya*, June 12, 2006.

"Ramadan Bomb Targets Shiites," *The Toronto Star*, September 24, 2006, p. A13.

Rathmell, Andrew, Olga Oliker, Terrence K. Kelly, David Brannan, and Keith Crane, *Developing Iraq's Security Sector: The Coalition Provisional Authority's Experience*, Santa Monica, Calif.: RAND Corporation, MG-365-OSD, 2005. As of May 22, 2007:
http://www.rand.org/pubs/monographs/MG365/

Ridolfo, Kathleen, "Iraq: Is Al-Sadr Stirring the Pot or Promoting Peace?" *Radio Free Europe/Radio Liberty*, February 28, 2006. As of April 12, 2007:
http://www.rferl.org/featuresarticle/2006/02/
8539708a-c6de-47e2-8bdd-d6d725b35632.html

Semple, Kirk, "In Victory for Shiite Leader, Iraqi Parliament Approves Creating Autonomous Regions," *The New York Times*, October 12, 2006, p. A12.

Tavernise, Sabrina, "Iraq Suspends Police Brigade in Baghdad," *The New York Times*, October 5, 2006, p. A14.

UN—*see* United Nations.

UNDP—*see* United Nations Development Programme.

UNHCR—*see* United Nations High Commissioner for Refugees.

United Nations, *General Framework Agreement for Peace in Bosnia and Herzegovina*, New York: United Nations, 1995.

United Nations Development Programme, *Iraq Living Conditions Survey 2004*, Baghdad, Iraq: Central Organization for Statistics and Information Technology, Ministry of Planning and Development Cooperation, 2005.

United Nations High Commissioner for Refugees, "Iraq," undated Web page. As of April 12, 2007:
http://www.unhcr.org/country/irq.html

U.S. Central Intelligence Agency, "Tunisia," *The CIA World Fact Book*, Washington, D.C.: Central Intelligence Agency, annually since 1997, last updated March 15, 2007.

U.S. Department of Defense, *Measuring Stability and Security in Iraq: Report to Congress in Accordance with the Department of Defense Appropriations Act 2006 (Section 9010)*, Washington, D.C.: U.S. Department of Defense, November 2006. As of April 12, 2007:
http://www.defenselink.mil/pubs/pdfs/9010Quarterly-Report-20061216.pdf

U.S. Department of State, "Iraq Weekly Status Report," Washington, D.C.: Bureau of Near Eastern Affairs, U.S. Department of State, 2005–2007. As of February 26, 2007:
http://www.state.gov/p/nea/rls/rpt/iraqstatus/

U.S. Institute of Peace, "Peace Agreements Digital Collection: Croatia—The Erdut Agreement," November 12, 1995. As of April 17, 2007:
http://www.usip.org/library/pa/croatia/croatia_erdut_11121995.html

U.S. Joint Chiefs of Staff, *Joint Doctrine for Military Operations Other Than War*, Washington, D.C.: Joint Chiefs of Staff, JP 3-07, June 16, 1995. As of April 12, 2007:
http://purl.access.gpo.gov/GPO/LPS24910

Walker, David M., *Stabilizing Iraq: An Assessment of the Security Situation: Testimony for the Subcommittee on National Security, Emerging Threats and International Relations, House Committee on Government Reform*, Washington, D.C.: U.S. Government Accountability Office, GAO-06-1094T, September 11, 2006. As of April 12, 2007:
http://purl.access.gpo.gov/GPO/LPS76615

White House, "President's Address to the Nation," Washington, D.C., December 18, 2005. As of February 20, 2007:
http://www.whitehouse.gov/news/releases/2005/12/20051218-2.html

———, "Remarks by the President at Bob Corker for Senate and Tennessee Republican Party Dinner," Washington, D.C., August 30, 2006a. As of February 20, 2007:
http://www.whitehouse.gov/news/releases/2006/08/20060830-7.html

———, "Press Conference by the President," Washington, D.C., October 25, 2006b. As of February 20, 2007:
http://www.whitehouse.gov/news/releases/2006/10/20061025.html

Windawi, Ali, and Julian E. Barnes, "Violence Surges in Contested City of Kirkuk," *Los Angeles Times*, July 20, 2006, p. A5.

Wong, Edward, and Paul von Zielbauer, "Iraq Stumbling in Bid to Purge Rogue Officers," *The New York Times*, September 17, 2006, p. A1.

Youssef, Nancy A., "Sectarian Suspicion Plagues Iraqi Army," McClatchy-Tribune News Service, August 18, 2006.

Youssef, Nancy A., and Mohammed al Dulaimy, "Shiites Flee After Sunni Threats," *The Seattle Times*, September 25, 2005. As of April 12, 2007:
http://seattletimes.nwsource.com/html/nationworld/2002519078_iraqcleanse25.html

Zavis, Alexandra, "U.S. Hopes to Build Iraqi Police Force," Associated Press, April 23, 2006.